GETTING UP TO SPEED

○○○○○○○○○○○○○○○○○○○○○○○○○○○○○○○○○○○○

GETTING UP TO SPEED

○ ○

*115 Quick Tips for
the New or Future Manager*

GEORGE J. LUMSDEN

American Management Association

New York • Atlanta • Boston • Chicago • Kansas City • San Francisco • Washington, D.C.
Brussels • Toronto • Mexico City

This publication is designed to provide accurate and authoritative information in regard to the subject matter covered. It is sold with the
understanding that the publisher is not engaged in rendering legal,
accounting, or other professional service. If legal advice or other expert
assistance is required, the services of a competent professional person
should be sought.

Library of Congress Cataloging-in-Publication Data

Lumsden, George J.
    Getting up to speed : 115 quick tips for the new or future manager
/ George J. Lumsden.
        p.   cm.
    Includes index.
    ISBN 0-8144-7789-5
    1. Management.   I. Title.
HD31.L77   1992
658—dc20   92-23822
                                                                  CIP

Printing number

10   9   8   7   6   5   4   3   2

To
Marge,
whose contribution to management
has been to raise two and encourage others . . .
a job well done.

○ ○

Contents

Part Three
Choosing a Management Style 61

Part Four
Communications: A Management Tool   *91*

Part Five
Management Skills and Behavior   *117*

Part Six
Effective Relationships on the Job   *153*

○ ○ ○ ○ ○ ○ ○ ○ ○ ○ ○ ○ ○ ○ ○ ○ ○ ○ ○

Introduction

A friend of mine used to say to new managers, "Being at the top is nice, but the real fun is in getting there!" I saw some inspirational value in that idea, so one day I borrowed the line in making a presentation to some harried managers. From the back of the room I heard someone mutter, "As long as you think getting kicked in the teeth is fun!"

Sure, it isn't easy. I would guess that no manager—at the top or anywhere in the middle—would describe the process as simple or painless. But the fact remains that each step up is a victory of its own, and when you learn how to master new skills and develop new self-confidence, you can't help but find enjoyment in it.

Even the best business schools don't put their graduates off the end of the knowledge assembly line fully equipped to be managers. Nor do corporate training programs fill in all the voids. Formal education and training can get you on track, but getting up to speed is *your* responsibility.

Another thing. What I've discovered, after making the trek myself and in helping others get off to a running start, is that it's not the big things that cause the headaches but odds and ends: seldom used skills, street smarts, and horse sense. These are the elements that often make one person succeed while another fails or plateaus out far below his or her expectations.

Events of recent years have put pressures on managers not only to succeed but to survive. Some of us who have butted heads against corporate walls for years are stunned by the unpredictability of modern business. Reorganizations, downsizings, mergers and acquisitions, cost reductions, and the introduction of new technology are changing management jobs and eliminating some altogether. Economists and business gurus tell us not to expect a return to the old multilayered and highly compartmentalized corporate structures of the past.

We used to contend that rising in management was difficult because the funnel gets narrower at the top. Well, get ready for the news: Funnels are now a bit narrow at the bottom too. If you're going to survive, succeed, or have fun as a manager, you had better prepare yourself as carefully as possible. Maybe this book will help in that preparation.

What's here won't give you all the know-how, skills, or street smarts you need—just some quick ideas that may help you cope with a number of fairly common concerns of beginning managers as they simultaneously wrestle with new challenges and strive to rise in the organizational hierarchy. I've identified these concerns in some thirty-eight years of managing and training managers in corporate life and as a management training consultant. I've watched some issues change and some remain the same. What goes around comes around—except when it flies out of orbit!

By design, the following 115 chapters are short and treat a number of subjects almost at random. I mentioned odds and ends earlier—that's what you'll find here. Because the chapters are short and independent of each other, you can begin anywhere and go in any direction. For those who prefer structure, or who are seeking immediate help with a particular kind of problem, I have arranged the pieces in six basic categories:

1. The Manager and the Organization
2. Motivating Others
3. Choosing a Management Style
4. Communications: A Management Tool
5. Management Skills and Behavior
6. Effective Relationships on the Job

Finding the fun in getting there in management is much like finding fun when you first learned to ride a two-wheeled bike. Until you learned how to *get up to speed*—and *stay there*—riding a bike amounted to little more than scraped knees and bumped elbows. So now that you know that, pedal hard and have a nice ride!

○ ○

Part One

The Manager and the Organization

There's a certain redundancy when we speak of managers *and* organizations, because one doesn't exist without the other. What gives meaning to any discussion of managers and their organizations is how each relates to the other and what both can accomplish together.

What is a manager? What is a manager expected to do? Can a manager succeed without a sense of mission or a proprietary attitude? How does a manager affect an organization, and vice versa? What is this business about corporate climates? What defines leadership? How does a manager deal effectively with in-house politics?

Do managers see budgets as working tools or as annual grab bags? How about reorganizations and cutbacks? How free are managers to do what they please? Given a choice, how should a manager pick a role model? Or are there any? Are managers agents of change or guardians of the status quo? These questions are deadly serious in the quest to become a better manager.

Organizations exist because the work to be done is more extensive or more complex than one person can handle. Managers exist because organizations need direction and control. Unless managers see those relationships, it's unlikely that they'll function in the balanced best interest of companies, employees, or themselves.

This section presents some ideas about dealing with these issues.

○ ○ ○ ○ ○ ○ ○ ○ ○ ○ ○ ○ ○ ○ ○ ○ ○ ○ ○ ○

1

The Manager: A Perspective

If you were to look up the word *manage* in the dictionary, you'd see many definitions. For example:

"To bring about or succeed in accomplishing"
"To have charge of or responsibility for"
"To handle, direct, govern, or control"

These are all upbeat definitions and reflect the common perceptions of managing. Now try this one:

"To continue to function despite hardship or difficulty, or to get along"

It's the unusual manager who isn't in the last category at some time or another. Maybe it's the Peter Principle—promotions may have taken you too far and too fast, and you've reached your own level of incompetence. Maybe it's an unusual set of circumstances—a new boss whose ideas and attitudes require considerable adjustment on your part or whose personality is difficult to cope with. Or maybe it's an employee whose behavior is not to your liking.

Whatever the reason, functioning in the face of hardship is the most uncomfortable state in which you can find yourself. It's also the condition top management doesn't appreciate in managers at any level. Managers who succeed are those who can dig themselves out of a hole and become thoroughly take-charge, make-things-happen managers—or even better, who can keep themselves from getting into holes in the first place.

Successful managers put their roles into proper perspective. You need to consider the job, the players who surround you—superiors and subordinates—the corporate climate in which you perform, and the tools with which you can do the job. These are the relationships—personal and physical—that outline the job ahead.

Particularly important is taking stock of yourself and what's happening around you. The issue is not how hard you work but how well you do it. Are you moving along or just getting along? Are you taking hold, or are you being told? Are you the generator of change or the inheritor of it? Are your ideas accepted topside, or are they ignored? Do your subordinates accept your direction *willingly* or *reluctantly?*

Successful managers make things happen—and smoothly. Anticipate business needs, and uncover ways to satisfy them. Don't fight fires; prevent them. You'll rise to the top if you stay on top of things. You'll be respected by superiors, liked by peers, and followed by subordinates.

Putting your role into proper perspective isn't always easy, but it's always necessary. And however jarring you may find any experience, you'll also find it helpful in guiding you to a successful future.

○ ○ ○ ○ ○ ○ ○ ○ ○ ○ ○ ○ ○ ○ ○ ○ ○ ○ ○

2

Larger
Than Life

Someone recently observed that back in the 1940s and 1950s—and even earlier—life tried to imitate the movies. Then, in the 1960s, 1970s, and 1980s, the movies tried to imitate life. Unfortunately, when it comes to portraying business characters, current movies and television seem to make managers larger than life.

Why? Because if managers were depicted on the silver screen as they really are, people would stay away in droves. Also, scriptwriters are men and women who probably have never spent a day in an office, a factory, a warehouse, or a sales territory. What difference does it make to them if they produce caricatures instead of characters?

Most management, unlike the movie image, consists of the routine daily handling of problems. What makes management—and managers—interesting is the nature of the problems and the manner in which those problems are solved. Having worked directly for two of *Fortune's* Top Ten and functioned in an agency relationship with others in or near that class, I have yet to meet men and women such as those I see and hear courtesy of the networks (or the nutworks). My guess is that the Hollywood versions wouldn't make it in real life. More important, no manager who patterned himself or herself on that level would last very long.

Managers get paid to think, to identify problems or foresee and prevent them, to use interpersonal relationships to work effectively up and down and across an organization, to guide others to work efficiently and in line with corporate objectives. They may be assertive and even aggressive, but they can't walk all over people. They may be precise, even demanding, but they have to match their demands with honest help for those who have to do the work.

Management is a responsibility, not a privilege. It requires a commitment to the work, not merely to getting ahead. It is judged on results, not fancy footwork. Sure, there are a few managers who don't feel that way or work that way; you'll always find exceptions who will slip through the net. If you are surrounded by many who operate that way, you're in the wrong outfit.

If you have time, enjoy a movie or turn on the TV. But don't expect to learn much about real-world management from the heroes or villains you see there.

○ ○

3

Corporate Cultures

The term is relatively new, but the concept has been around a long time. *Corporate culture* describes the overall "feel" of a business organization. Some companies are relaxed, some uptight. Some are people oriented; others aim at productivity at all costs and consider personnel little more than components in the process. Some regularly reward performance, and others wait until cornered by individuals or the union.

Some organizations thrive on rumor and conflict and applaud aggressiveness. Others set up entire departments to stimulate communications within the organization and quash internal bickering, and they take a dim view of ruthless climbers. There are companies where quality is paramount, and companies where quality is what you get sometimes.

Organization size is not always the critical factor determining culture. There are small companies with a sterile environment and large corporations with a family atmosphere. Go into the offices of any company, and, sooner or later, you'll get a fairly good reading on its overall corporate culture.

Owners or top management sets the corporate culture, and that style filters down through the organization. It can be changed; sometimes there is an enclave within the city walls. That change does take courage and tremendous imagination.

Let's suppose, for instance, that you work for a hard-nosed, noncaring, top-down management, and you want to stay on because it offers you the best opportunity. But you want to develop a team or participative management style and get high quality and productivity in a manner uncommon in your company. Move slowly and quietly, and do it. The folks upstairs will never know, but they'll surely admire your bottom line.

Corporate culture begets loyalty or generates employee turnover. Some people fit well in one culture and poorly in another. If you're comfortable with your company's culture, you'll want to stay with it and surround yourself with others who'll fit in it. If you're not, you'll have to learn to like it or prepare your résumé. Or risk changing the organization.

○ ○

4

A Sense of Ownership

A very successful businessman, who had owned and run some profitable businesses in his time, recently remarked that if one were to look for exceptional businesspeople, the last place to look would be a major corporation. I readily agreed with him but didn't let it go at that. I asked him why he felt that way.

"The trouble with corporate life," my friend said, "is that everything gets very compartmentalized. A manager heads a department, and that localizes his or her concern to that department's activity. Period. If you're in sales, don't meddle with personnel. If you're in personnel, don't start poking around in sales. That's true in any set of corporate functions. Organizational structure and protocol dictate that. It's the way it works best in large companies."

"But that makes for greater expertise in a given field and for improved efficiency in the overall organization, doesn't it?" I asked.

A pained expression came over his face as I asked the question. "Expertise, yes. Efficiency, no. That's fine if you're talking about high tech, and you have to have specific expertise to handle it. But what we're talking about is business-oriented thinking, and the average manager doesn't do enough of that."

Our discussion went on. We concluded that top managers *owe* lower-level managers information and insight into the vital problems of the business. For their part, lower-level managers should inquire, pay attention, and explore business needs at whatever level they can. Finally, we agreed that managers in big companies *owe* the company a sense of ownership—in other words, they must manage each department as if it were a company within a company. Not bad advice.

There are, to their credit, many managers who take a proprietary interest in their companies. And there are managers whose sense of ownership extends only as far as the ends of their noses. If you want to succeed as a manager, you'd better follow the first course.

○ ○

5

A Sense of Mission— And a Plan

All great leaders have a sense of mission. They have in mind a grand plan for themselves and for their organizations. This is true whether the leader is the president of the company or the manager of a department.

True leaders are not content with the status quo; they keep asking themselves what they can do next to make their operation run better, faster, more economically, or more profitably. By contrast, followers are perfectly content to keep their heads down and pursue those courses someone else has laid out for them. Oh, and they must be both comfortable and safe.

Much of the management literature emphasizes the adroit maneuver that moves one above the pack. But great leaders are more than good maneuverers. They also have ideas and plans and the courage to make them fly. In short, they offer something better.

Missions require planning. Wild ideas remain wild unless there has been some careful thought about getting them under control and into a workable form. Merely to say that you want something isn't enough. You have to know the steps needed to get what you want and be able to predictably harness the elements at your disposal. Dream a little and think a lot.

Let's suppose you are the head of your department. Is your mission merely to review reports of what's happening, sign papers, pass along information to top management, and go home at the end of the day? If so, your department and your company are in deep trouble, because standing still in today's business environment is actually falling behind.

Now let's suppose you are a first-level manager in a department with others who are equal or senior in rank. You have your particular operation going smoothly. Is that all you have in mind to do? Or do you see a way to make your contribution more vital to the overall success of your company? Do you see an internal improvement that, if put into effect, would make a difference in improved productivity and cost effectiveness? That may be perceived as your mission.

Just wishing won't turn good ideas into reality. To the noble mission must be added the shirtsleeves planning that makes it real. And even if the mission you entertain isn't for today, begin the planning nevertheless. When the time comes, you'll be ready to go. That's leadership.

○ ○

6

Making It Fit— Not Having a Fit

If you were going to design a machine, you would first get a firm idea of what that machine is supposed to do and then draw a rough design of what that machine might look like. Where possible, you would specify using readily available parts—no sense in inventing something when what you need is already at hand. Tight plans would follow, then a working model, and so on.

The same sequence is true of designing an organization. First, you determine what that organization is supposed to accomplish; then rough up an organization chart and look around for people to fit into the squares. If you're lucky, most of the people are on hand, but you still have to fit those people into the newly drawn squares. What do you do next?

Admittedly, new managers aren't often faced with developing a totally new organization. More frequently, they are faced with departmental expansion—or contraction. In either case, what was once considered a working organization no longer fits the work that must be done. There are new responsibilities for added personnel or added responsibilities for those left.

This so-called new organization requires redefining the parts that are supposed to fit into it. And that means redesigning job descriptions . . . not all, perhaps, but some. Job descriptions aren't lists of tasks to be performed but delineations of responsibilities and accountabilities. These sections should be included:

- Position/title
- Overall objectives/functions
- Reporting relationships
- Responsibilities
- Authority
- Performance standards/accountability

The more general the statements are, the more latitude you have in assigning and controlling. Avoid the temptation to write a laundry list of tasks and procedures.

When you face the task of redefining roles in your department, make sure the fit of people and responsibilities is good—or you may have a fit in trying to manage them.

○ ○

7

What's a Person Like You Doing in a Place Like This?

One of the old gags in a company I once worked for went like this: Question: "How many people work over there?" Answer: "About half of them."

The truth is that in many companies, people are underemployed. Jobs are created, and people are hired to fill them. Work is assigned, and it gets done. But there's more to it than that. The following questions must always be kept in mind:

- Are some people carrying too large a load?
- Are some people carrying too little a load?
- Could some jobs be folded into other jobs?
- Could some jobs be done away with altogether?

Some of the best work I ever did was accomplished without benefit of a job description. The reason was simple: the organization was small, we had distinct specialties, and we all worked overtime to handle the load. In emergencies, we doubled for one another but otherwise stayed clear of the other person's sandbox. You can do that in small organizations. But in the standard corporation, job descriptions are necessary. More often than not, though, after they are written, they are filed and all but forgotten. Sometimes an individual's actual work bears little or no resemblance to the job description for that job. Perhaps responsibilities have been added or taken away; lines of reporting have changed; performance standards have been raised or lowered; authority once granted has been taken away or, worse, authority not originally accorded has been assumed.

I joined an organization as a manager and was told that job descriptions were in place. The trouble was, I couldn't find them in the files, so, one by one, I called my employees in for a short conference. "Please bring your job description with you," I requested. Some couldn't find them; others brought in documents that were yellow with age. The truth was that nobody had a functional description.

Together we rewrote the descriptions. We included position/title, overall objectives and functions, reporting relationships, responsibilities and spelled-out authority, and performance standards. Each person knew what he or she was expected to do.

Have you looked at your employees' job descriptions lately? Have you looked at your own? Accurate, up-to-date job descriptions are tools for better management. Not only do they help *you*, but they help the individual for whom they were written.

○ ○

8

Let's Try Something Different

If you plan to introduce change in your organization, realize right now that you'll meet resistance. Why? Change threatens. Change confuses. Change requires work.

One of the classic management mistakes occurs when a new manager is assigned to take over a department. Perhaps the old manager has retired or has been promoted, and now you come along expecting to make things hum. Indeed, there may be some pressure on you to bring about changes. Perhaps you were told bluntly, "Go down there and get things cracking." You might even have some specific instructions on what to do and how to do it.

Do you go into the new position on Monday morning and call a meeting of the staff and say, "I'm here to get things cracking"? Not if you value your life and career, you don't. Rather than attempt to bring about an overnight conversion of the department and the people in it, move as though you were walking through a dense thicket known to have swallowed up pioneers.

Here are five ideas for bringing about change in such a situation. The ideas are simple, even if executing them isn't:

1. Get to know people first. You'll discover who the leaders and gripers are. Start with staff, and then move deeper into the organization.
2. Find out what people do and whether they're happy doing it. Find out what things they feel might be done differently. You probably won't even have to ask.
3. Hold private meetings with key personnel after you have a reasonably good picture of what's going on in the organization. Sow the seeds of change, and develop both understanding and commitment. Counsel. Don't insist.
4. Let others bring about the changes *you* want because *they* want to do it. This takes longer than if you were to give absolute direction, but it works better.
5. Give credit where it is due.

Some of the changes you want to make are those others may have wanted to make for a long time. Managing is more than giving orders; it is getting things done through others. Why not manage change that way?

9

A Sense of Security

Labor unions have placed steadily growing importance on the subject of job security. Managers often consider this to be a working-class effort toward the establishment of a sinecure that would, in effect, tie the hands of management. Such managers say, "Give 'em job security, and they'll take advantage of it with less and less productivity."

That could be true. Some people surely would take advantage of security. But it doesn't have to be that way. Most people, properly advised, work with equal skill, care, and effort knowing that if they do so, they can count on steady employment and a weekly paycheck.

Ironically, some of the managers who looked askance at the job security issue quickly became proponents of it when their own security was threatened because of mergers, acquisitions, and general corporate downsizing. They thought they were safe until Black Friday, when they were advised that their services were no longer needed.

Security is a motivator, and an important one at that. The job for managers is to communicate to their subordinates the idea that security is earned, just as money, respect, and other human needs are earned.

We earn security with quality. We earn it with customer service. We earn it with cost-effectiveness. We earn it by obeying corporate policies and procedures. We earn it by being on the job regularly and on time. We earn it by taking an attitude that what is good for the company ultimately translates into benefits for the individual.

Even if you control the destiny of just a small department, your role is to convey these ideas. Set high-quality standards and monitor them. Hold customer service in high regard, and let it be known that you do. Set examples of behavior and demonstrate loyalty up, down, and across the organization. You may not be able to promise security, but you can help put it into proper perspective for those under your supervision.

○ ○

10

Today
We Reorganize

If it hasn't already happened in your company, keep a weather eye peeled for it. Corporate reorganization is the current fad, and it's causing both hardship and embarrassment. The truth is that many organizations have grown fat, and massive efforts at cost reduction are ubiquitous in the corporate world.

The empire builders among us have been laid bare. We now discover that Department A doesn't need twenty-nine employees but can be just as productive with seventeen. To the corporate directive to get rid of 10 percent of the heads, Manager A complied. First went the clerical people. With nobody to handle the paperwork generated by all the others, the paperwork diminished. Then Manager A discovered that this report, and then that report, weren't needed. And so it went.

Initial cuts in employment are often done with an axe. Later, to handle the fine cutting necessary to meet second- and third-wave personnel reductions, a scalpel is used. Axe wielding is simple, but it takes real dexterity to handle a scalpel. You'd better be up to it.

If you are in this position, analyze the various functions under your supervision. Take a hard look at personnel to see who can double in brass and who needs retraining. Understand what Parkinson's Law is all about: Work expands to fill the time available for its completion—or people assigned to it.

Say you had seven people reporting to you, and now you have five. How do you reassign the work of the two who have been outplaced without disrupting the overall productivity of the department? How do you downgrade individuals and change reporting relationships without turning the whole building into a zoo? Can rank and function be seen in a different way?

And occasionally in reorganizational efforts, managers come up with not fewer but more personnel. If that happens to you, are you ready for it?

○ ○

11

If It's Not Here, It's on Its Way

There are new winds blowing in the management field—some of them gentle and others of hurricane force that have blown many managers out of their secure little roosts. These winds are called "trim the overhead."

The news came as a shock to Ted. He thought he was secure at his company; it never occurred to him that they could do without him. But his department and Bill's group were merged, and Ted ended up as odd man out. Oh, they cut Ted a nice severance package, and he found a reasonably respectable job elsewhere, but things weren't the same.

Ted should have seen it coming. It began six years ago. At first, the winds blew away some of Ted's clerical help. No more typed letters or interdepartmental memos—just short, handwritten notes and telephone calls. Then came the banks of computer terminals. The monthly summaries Ted's department had prepared with care became unnecessary; the computer was not only up to date but up to the minute. Ted saw electronics as his enemy.

Ted's former boss contended that Ted had built himself a sinecure and had given up being creative and productive long ago. Ted had built himself a reputation as being resistant to change and accepted it only when it was forced upon him.

Bill, on the other hand, had initiated change and capitalized on it. The work done in Bill's department was increasingly reflected on the bottom line, and the work done in Ted's wasn't. The two departments overlapped some. The topside decision was to combine them and trim the overhead.

But what really did Ted in was the fact that his cover was blown when he lost personnel in his little department. Ted was a pretender. He was the compleat delegator, and when he was forced to dismiss his subordinates, he stood naked in the town square! They had known more than he did.

There are a lot of Teds in this world . . . or there were. Businesses used to be able to support a whole gaggle of midlevel supervisors who took up a little slack, helped move the work forward a bit, and seldom demonstrated a capacity to initiate but were handy. No more. Staffs are getting leaner, and only the more productive folks are still around.

In order to stick around today, be a *manager:* Maximize productivity, hound quality, effect forward movement through dedicated effort within the work group, and minimize frictions outside it. There are no more free lunches, no more easy rides, no more good old Teds. Before the winds blow your way, be ready for them.

○ ○

12

What Price Visibility?

"Every time I go into Sam's office, he's on the phone. What gives, anyhow?"

"Haven't you heard? Sam was just made president of Rotary Club, and he gets lots of calls from committee chairs."

"I've been looking for Mary all week. Is she out of town on business?"

"No. Mary just got tagged with representing the company on the United Fund campaign. She'll be tied up from now until the thing's over."

Many companies encourage managers to become involved in community affairs. A good performance by a manager in highly visible civic roles is effective public relations for the company. Additionally, benefits can accrue to the individual who is willing to serve in worthwhile activities. But there is a price for such visibility.

The point is not to discourage involvement but to face up to the balance between costs and benefits. By adding to a work load, there is the risk of not getting the regular job done. Or if the job does get done, does it get done well? Or if it does get done well, does such effort subtract from one's health and personal freedom?

Something has to give. The old saying "If you want a job done, give it to a busy person" probably hides a real truth: Busy people who are able to get extra things done are those who are well organized and can cut enough corners to handle both sides of the situation without sacrificing either.

Are the people you supervise well enough trained to pick up some of your in-office work when you do community work? Can you organize the outside function and delegate work to others? Can you arrange to have outside activities not interfere with normal work hours—or to interfere as little as possible? Can you change hats quickly and easily without getting flustered? Will your family and friends recognize your added work load and schedule their activities around them? Will your health support additional physical, mental, and emotional pressure?

By all means take on high-visibility roles—if you can answer all of those questions affirmatively. The key is to have your own job under full control so that you can handle more.

○ ○ ○ ○ ○ ○ ○ ○ ○ ○ ○ ○ ○ ○ ○ ○ ○ ○ ○ ○

13

Preparing for the Presidency

Put your political mind at ease; I'm not going to lay out a road map to the White House. Instead, let's explore what has to take place in your self-development if the title *president* appears anywhere on your agenda.

Typically, accession to the top levels of any company is done by a process known as "going through the chairs." One look at many major corporations tells us that some executives go through the chairs more slowly than others. Another look tells us that it's possible not to sit in all the chairs on the way to the top. So there must be something about how you can prepare for elevation in a business organization.

People who become CEOs learn a lot about things other than their own specialty. Although they may begin as financial people, they have to know a lot about marketing. If they begin as engineers, they have to get a good grasp on finance, personnel, and sales. Whatever you know best isn't enough. You have to know some of what others know, too. Broadening begins within the organization. But that's not where it ends.

Top managers, and especially presidents, need an understanding of other businesses with which they interface, of national and international finance, and of political systems, and they must be able to move comfortably in a variety of situations. They find themselves giving speeches, being interviewed on radio and television and for the newspapers, and writing for publication.

So keep up with national and international affairs. Pay attention to banking and the stock markets. Make sure you have a fair knowledge of law and economics. Develop your command of the English language and your ability to express yourself in speech and in writing.

Certainly presidents have a lot of insulation, with public relations departments close at their heels, but when it comes to facing the press or the public, they can't delegate the right-now responsibility to someone else. The broader their knowledge and the sharper their skills, the more successful they are in the role.

This is not an overnight crash course. It's a long-term development. If you're aiming for the top, the time to start is now.

○ ○ ○ ○ ○ ○ ○ ○ ○ ○ ○ ○ ○ ○ ○ ○ ○ ○ ○ ○

14

The Problem
With Politics

More than one manager has said, "I like the work here, but the politics stink." More than one manager has quit his or her job because politics was so troublesome. Oddly enough, some companies discourage politics, and others seem to foster it. But in either case, politics exists.

In its finest sense, politics means working within the system. In its worst sense, it means seeking advancement or power or getting credit not deserved. Many managers find these things difficult to handle. And because they find it difficult, clever politicians take full advantage of them.

To be politic means to be sagacious, prudent, judicious, and expedient, as well as to be shrewd and artful. Maybe you deplore the craftiness of some of your peers, but in order to survive, you have to become a bit street smart yourself. That doesn't mean you play the other guy's game, but it does mean you have to know how to avoid it or defend against it.

Morgan was a master at currying the boss's favor, and he had been given raises and an embellished title. Morgan didn't have the talent to back it up, but no matter; he hung in there by dumping some of his more difficult tasks on Sandra, who was not his subordinate but a fairly new kid on the block. One day Sandra announced that she was leaving to take a job elsewhere. Unfortunately for Morgan, she was in the midst of a job Morgan had been assigned but that was beyond his understanding. His incompetence was revealed, and his boss finally saw it. Politics couldn't save Morgan.

Marsha was competent, but she'd been told long ago that one moved faster with political support. She affiliated herself as closely as possible with Liz, her boss, with the single objective of being carried aloft on Liz's magic carpet. By doing so, Marsha unknowingly inherited the wrath of Liz's opponents, and Liz had a few in the shop. The upshot was that promotions that might have come Marsha's way went elsewhere; she had joined a losing political party.

There is legitimate politicking. It includes anticipating your boss's need for assistance, being willing to take on work that saves him or her time and effort, recommending actions that are beneficial and in which you can play a role, and demonstrating loyalty in an honest way. You're at your political best when you're doing your job well. You're at your political worst when you fawn and toady and play corporate doormat.

Watch for subordinates who play political games with you. They make you feel good at the moment, but not so good when you discover you've been used. Politics isn't everybody's game, and we may be better off if it isn't played at all. Watch destructive politics, and steer clear of it.

○ ○

15

Keeping Peace in the Family

We tend to think of customers as people *out there*—those who buy our products or services and therefore deserve our greatest care and effort. True, those who buy from us provide us with revenue, and our obligation to them is vital. But what about the "families" within our own company? They deserve some consideration, too.

By "families within" I'm referring to the departments in a company. Too often, adversarial relationships develop among them. The sales department feels that the personnel department isn't cooperating, the manufacturing department doesn't feel that purchasing is doing a good job, and accounting believes it could work better if engineering would only cooperate.

This sort of infighting normally develops over misunderstandings that could be deflected easily if the managers involved stepped up to them. Left unattended, little problems blow up into major ones. On the other hand, when affected managers get together to solve mutual headaches, the result often is bonding that is mutually beneficial.

Sales and service are excellent examples of potential clash. Salespeople say that their customers aren't cared for on time and satisfactorily, so repeat business is difficult to attain. For their part, service contends that salespeople in their territory sell customers the wrong equipment or make outlandish claims for it. So instead of working together to satisfy customers, sales and service work against each other. Even worse, they sometimes lay these problems off on customers.

Bill Richards, the sales manager, went to Chris Walsh, the service manager. "Chris," he said, "we have a mutual problem. My reps tell me that some of their sales are made especially difficult because of customer service. Now I'm sure that your service reps have similar criticisms of some of our sales practices. Let's talk about it."

Chris replied, "That's right, Bill. ABC Company is a good case in point. We've repaired their equipment a dozen times. We can't tell them that they should have had a bigger unit to begin with, and they're working it too hard, but that's the case in a nutshell. Now the situation at XYZ Company is another matter; we fouled that one up with an inexperienced rep doing the installation. It's time we worked this out together. I'm open to suggestions if you are."

Open discussion between department managers can keep peace in the family and keep the neighborhood happy. All it takes is two people facing up to common problems without pointing fingers at each other.

○ ○

16

It's Not All That Important

"Let Sam handle that . . . it's not all that important."

"Just write the guy a note and sign my name . . . it's not all that important."

"Don't bother to look it up; just give an approximate figure . . . it's not all that important."

If ever you hear yourself saying, "It's not all that important," envision a red flag in front of you. Labeling anything unimportant may be the biggest mistake you can make. "Unimportant" things can bite you when you aren't looking.

Watch the golf pros. *Nothing* is unimportant to them. They line up a ten-inch putt as carefully as they do a ten-footer. What they know is that missing a short one costs them as much as missing a long one. And one stroke often costs them as much money as six or seven strokes in a close tournament.

Bill used to get a lot of correspondence across his desk. On particularly busy days, he'd say to his secretary, "This pile isn't important, so send them our standard form letter. Sign my name." That wouldn't have been so bad if Bill hadn't read the incoming mail so hurriedly. One day a memo came from a new customer who had a serious point to make. And that customer had a private pipeline to the top reaches of Bill's company.

Maria was asked to give a short report at a management meeting on the activities in her department. She was busy at other things she thought were more important and decided she could do the report pretty much off the top of her head. She arrived at the meeting with a few hastily scrawled notes and absolutely no rehearsal—only to discover the room filled with top brass whose purpose was to review budgets and staff requirements. She suffered immediate embarrassment. Worse, she didn't get the money and manpower she needed.

Woody was asked to look over a report and buck it back to his boss ASAP with comments. It wasn't all that important, Woody determined, so he scanned the material, penciled a couple of sloppy stick-on notes here and there, and sent it back to the boss with a cover note that said, "Looks okay to me." His boss sent it back upstairs because he too thought it not all that important. You guessed it. Someone up in the sanctum sanctorum found the stick-ons, and it wasn't a barrel of fun!

To be sure, not everything you confront on a typical business day is all that important. But even with unimportant items, exercise some care. Read more than the first line before you make a judgment. Write comments with the thought that someone important might read them. Prepare for casual presentations with the thought that you can dress them down easier than you can dress them up.

When you find yourself thinking that it's not all that important, take a second look to be sure.

○ ○

17

The Mark of Quality

More interest has been shown in quality recently than at any other time since World War II. The consumer movement has put industry as a whole on guard. Businesses that haven't responded to the challenge have suffered.

Quality can't be achieved with press releases; it has to be delivered. A young manager I know handled public relations for a large company. One day he was summoned into the president's office and directed to launch a press campaign on the company's quality program. "When will this program begin, and what is it?" inquired the young man. "Just tell them we have a program, and we'll catch up on it later on," snorted the president.

In checking with a number of key executives, the young manager confirmed his guess that this was a top-of-the-head judgment on the part of the president; nobody else knew anything about a quality program, either. Rather than prepare a press release, the young man updated his résumé. When he left the company sometime later, the quality drive still was a dream.

The experts contend that a program for quality improvement has to begin at the top. But in truth any manager can launch a quality movement. If you do, you will never be criticized for the work. And even if you are not directly connected with a product, you can still push for quality in your own service area. Accounting? Better and prompter reports. Sales? Better customer relationships. Purchasing? Closer control on vendors and the product they sell you.

The story goes that when Marshall Field was personally operating his famous Chicago store, he pulled off all labels indicating the manufacturer. His reason: "All people have to know is that if it was purchased at Marshall Field's, it has to be the best." His success was built on that type of credibility.

Quality begins with a commitment to set standards of performance. The responsibility for quality belongs at the most immediate level—the person who does the work, not an inspector who examines it later. Quality gets all hands aboard and paddling together.

○ ○

18

"Close Enough for Government Work"

It's a phrase that's been around for a number of years, though nobody seems to know how it started. It's used when referring to a job that doesn't come up to standards but presumably nobody will ever know the difference. Military personnel on the front line or astronauts on the launching pad would hardly agree with it. To them, "close enough for government work" means absolutely perfect.

There is quality—and there is quality. We buy products every day that are of lesser quality than other similar items of very high quality. Shoehorns laid out for guest use at hotels are made of plastic—functional, but not of superior quality. Shoehorns advertised in catalogs aimed at the carriage trade are identical in function but made of high-grade steel—more decorative and considerably more expensive. Obviously, more care and more expense is put into the manufacture of the latter.

The same could be said for inexpensive watches and transistor radios. If they serve the function and last a reasonable length of time, they're accepted as good-enough quality. A building contractor doesn't use first-grade lumber to rough in a building; he or she saves the good stuff for finishing the job. Quality differences are accepted in all businesses.

Quality begins with standards that are set with a clear understanding of the quality that will be accepted. A manager might say to a secretary, "Give me a rough type of this copy so that I can make changes in it. I need it in a hurry." Time becomes the criterion, and the secretary knows that a few typos will be tolerated. "Here is the corrected copy. It's going upstairs for final review, so please check it carefully," indicates a different level of quality. How the work is ordered sets the standards.

One thing is sure: Whenever work of substandard quality is accepted, you have set a new standard. That's true whether your concern is a product coming off the line or sales in a territory. Accept a bad finish, and you'll get bad finishes. Accept sales of 85 percent of objectives, and you'll live with that standard.

We may not always be looking for peak quality, but we must always set standards for the quality we want to achieve. "Close enough for government work," repeated often enough, ensures diminishing quality all along the line.

○ ○

19

Budgets and the Bottom Line

It's always important to bear in mind that when you set your budget in October for the following year, you are playing an important role in designing the profits that will show up when the books are closed fourteen months from now.

Unless you're the president of the company, you know that between your requests and what you finally get to operate on are a raft of evaluations and revisions—most of them by people who really don't understand what your department does anyhow. Many managers load up their budget submissions knowing they'll be cut back automatically. They ask for a million dollars, knowing that if they get $900,000, they'll be in clover.

Consider submitting your budget proposals by project. Make it clear to the upper-level manager who will take the first cut on your submission that by taking out x dollars, he or she loses programs 1 and 2. That's fundamental to your negotiating process—something for something. It's honest and it's practical, and it makes operating under a cut budget reasonably simple.

When you have to absorb budget cuts by, let's say, 10 percent across the board, you find yourself cutting quality out of each of the activities you'll be responsible for next year. And if reduced spending results in less departmental effectiveness, the losers are the company, the department—and you.

I worked for many years in a budget-cutting environment, and it wasn't fun. My initial response was to keep a stiff upper lip and proceed to do all I was committed to do . . . with less money. By cheapening a few programs, I recognized a slip in quality. If I recognized it, wasn't it possible that my management would notice it, too?

Submitting budgets on a line-item basis can avoid that problem. When asked why a given project wasn't being done, my answer was simply, "It isn't in the budget." I discovered that if a project was important enough to someone upstairs, the pot got sweetened somewhere later on.

The better the budget you set and the better you live by it, the more highly regarded you'll be by those who monitor and measure your performance.

○ ○ ○ ○ ○ ○ ○ ○ ○ ○ ○ ○ ○ ○ ○ ○ ○ ○ ○ ○

20

Save Yourself Poor

Times are tough around Big Company. An edict comes down from on high to cut all budgets by 10 percent. Len and Ben each head a section of Gwen's department. Both have equal budgets, although they have quite different responsibilities. When Gwen passes on the bad news, both agree to conform.

Len calls a meeting of his group and tells them, "Whatever you're doing right now, stop doing it until we get a handle on this mess. We have to cut 10 percent out of the budget, and I want to approve any future spending before it's done." Everyone is suitably impressed. People go back to their workstations, and the operation begins to slow down.

Ben also calls a meeting to give the section the overall picture. Then he brings his subordinates in one at a time and asks each, "What are you doing now that could be postponed without seriously damaging your operation?" Together they review projects, approving some and eliminating others.

When Gwen meets with her section heads a week later, she gets a feeling that both are in control of the situation. "We'll meet the objective," says Len. "We're working on it," says Ben. Gwen likes Len's positive attitude, but she's concerned about Ben's and meets with him later. "We're cutting out nonessentials as we see them," Ben says. "But there are a number of expenditures that have to be made if we're going to be effective at all." Gwen decides to keep an eye on Ben's operation.

At year-end, Len comes in with a savings of 20 percent. Ben comes in a bit short—only 8.5 percent. Len's saving spree has cut down a number of worthwhile activities. As a result, many deadlines have not been met, customer complaints are on the rise, and workers' morale is low.

Ben, on the other hand, has managed to accomplish most of what he had set out to do with the exception of a few pet projects that would have been beneficial but that could be put back into the program in the future. In Ben's section, one would have thought business was going on as usual.

Poor Len. He thought he was going to get a medal or a loving cup—at least a compliment from Gwen. Instead he was criticized for not meeting his work objectives. "Budgets," Gwen reminded him, "are meant to be used. If our objective were to save money, the best way to do it would be to go out of business." Enough said.

○ ○

Part Two

Motivating Others

Old-line managers seldom gave motivation a thought. Vested with power, they pushed, shoved, and threatened others to perform. The tyrants and czars of old couldn't make it in today's workplaces, though there are still some bland copies of them doing their best to try.

As America rose out of the Great Depression of the 1930s, so did a movement called behavioral science, stressing theories dealing with people in social settings (including work situations). Some of the old guard in business ignored the researchers as egg-headed academicians who would soon go away. Others felt they were simply troublemakers.

True, they were theorists, and sometimes practical people see theory as suitable in college classrooms but not worth much in the real world. But how did behavioral science theories come into being? Two ways: (1) Behavior was observed often enough to let the observer conclude that predictable results came out of certain repeated actions; or (2) beginning with an assumption, the assumption was tested enough to conclude that results of a given action were predictable.

Some behavioral science theories have come and gone. Others have stuck around and have changed the way managers think and, more important, how they motivate people and work with them.

You will be exposed to a little theory in the pieces to come—I hope enough to make the practical applications make sense!

○ ○ ○ ○ ○ ○ ○ ○ ○ ○ ○ ○ ○ ○ ○ ○ ○ ○ ○ ○

21

A Hasty Trip
Through Theoryland

Any discussion of behavioral science in the workplace begins with the Hawthorne studies, started when Elton Mayo and others in the Hawthorne plant of Western Electric Company began to study the effects of environment on productivity. Briefly, they made several improvements in working conditions for one group of workers and absolutely no improvements for a control group. They observed both groups equally.

Productivity rose with the group for which improvements were made. That, they had guessed, might be the case. But were they surprised when productivity rose equally in the control group for which nothing had been done! When they asked members of the control group why they produced more, the answer was, "Because you were paying attention to us." While more came out of the Hawthorne studies than that, just that alone tells you a lot about motivation!

Abraham Maslow's contribution to the knowledge of behavior is best known as the Hierarchy of Needs. This theory says that motivation is the satisfaction of needs, from the most basic to the more exotic.

Douglas McGregor put his theories squarely into the workplace with his Theory X and Theory Y ideas. His contribution made managers who read him think differently about workers than they had in the past.

Frederick Herzberg's motivational theories arose out of studies focused on the "satisfiers" and "dissatisfiers" in work life. Surprise, surprise: People were found to be more motivated by achievement, recognition, responsibility, and interesting work than they were by money, perks, and job security. And we all thought that if we gave Margie a new office with a window she'd forget our bad supervision and lousy work rules! Herzberg showed us that meaningful work beats giveaways and doodads.

These pioneers in the development of ideas about motivation laid the building blocks on which many recent efforts have been made. If you know little more about motivation than to pay attention to people, focus on giving them interesting work, notice what they do and tell them about it, reward them fairly, recognize that people change as do their needs and that you owe them as much as they owe you, you're on your way to becoming a better manager.

○ ○

22

What Motivation Really Means

One of your key responsibilities as a manager is to get your employees producing at their very best, not just some of the time but at all times. Doing that is no simple trick . . . unless, that is, you really understand what motivation really means.

The authorities agree on one thing: All motivation is self-motivation. We do things for two basic reasons: to get something or to keep from losing something. One manager I know says that he has that concept down pat; he tells his employees that if they do a good job today, they'll be kept on the payroll tomorrow. That type of motivation centers on fear of losing.

A more effective type of motivation focuses on the positive: what one gets as a result of what one does. The following definition of motivation has served me well for many years, and perhaps it will help you: Motivation is getting others to do what you want them to do because *they* want to do it.

People have a variety of hidden agendas—what they want out of life. Colleen works because she is saving to buy a new car. José works because he has a family to support. Charlie works past his retirement date because he likes to be in the company of old friends and associates. Helen works because she is proving to her family that she is competent and wants to be admired for her steady growth in her career. All these people are looking for quite different rewards—some tangible and others intangible.

Abraham Maslow, the distinguished behavioral scientist, pointed out that motivation is essentially the satisfaction of needs. We work to satisfy a need, and when that need is satisfied, it's no longer a motivator. Keep that in mind because many managers attempt to motivate by going over the same old ground and missing the point entirely.

Maslow arranged these needs in what is called the Hierarchy of Needs:

Need for self-actualization
Need for esteem
Need to belong and be loved
Need to be safe
Need for physical things

Begin at the bottom of this hierarchy. Physical things are what people need to survive—food, clothing, shelter. When they finally have something, their concerns turn to protecting what they have. Safety. Then they want acceptance by others. Belonging. And when they achieve that, they want to be respected. Esteem. Finally, being all you can be. Self-actualization. Motivation doesn't end at payday.

The first step in motivating people is to uncover their needs or hidden agendas. The second step is to show those same people how they can satisfy those needs by performing the job they have before them. When you do that, you're a first-class motivator.

○ ○ ○ ○ ○ ○ ○ ○ ○ ○ ○ ○ ○ ○ ○ ○ ○ ○ ○

23

X and Y

Nearly thirty years ago, Douglas McGregor wrote a book that changed a lot of thinking in the field of management, *The Human Side of Enterprise.* He presented two assumptions on human nature in relation to work: Theory X and Theory Y.

Theory X is the conventional view of the average worker. It says that people dislike work; they must be directed, coerced, and threatened to put forth effort; they avoid responsibility; and they prefer security above all. This fits many management attitudes to a T.

Theory Y, in contrast, assumes that people enjoy doing work, just as they enjoy play and rest. Further, people will exercise self-direction; they are self-starters and pursue objectives. They not only accept responsibility but seek it. They like to achieve.

You and I certainly know people who might fit into these categories. Of course, we put *ourselves* into the Theory Y classification. But that wasn't McGregor's point. His concern was to have managers look differently at the potential of people and the management style that would bring it out. Some have and some haven't.

Would you rather have X or Y people working for you? My own choice is to avoid X types. Theory X people are those who have worked under highly directive management. They dislike work because all they're ever given to do are *tasks.* They don't seek responsibility because they know it will be denied them. If I had Theory X workers, my job would be very difficult.

Theory X and Theory Y workers are created by the managers for whom they work. Want to turn a Theory X into a Theory Y? *Involve* that individual. Set goals together. Assign some minor responsibility, and see how it goes. Change the nature of direction so that the individual works more and more on his or her own. Compliment work well done. Generate in the worker a real desire for accomplishment. Then Theory Y will become a reality.

When X becomes Y, managers become leaders, not drivers.

○ ○

24

Correcting— And Motivating

Maslow's Hierarchy of Needs sounds as though all motivation is a matter of positives. It is. It begins with physical needs and moves on to security, acceptance, esteem, and self-actualization needs. Thoroughly upbeat. So how do you motivate when you call a subordinate on the carpet?

The need we're concerned about in this situation is esteem or ego. Nobody likes to be berated. More than that, nobody likes to be criticized publicly. While managers do the employee—and themselves—a lot of good by complimenting publicly, they do just the opposite by criticizing in front of others.

You're meeting with several of your subordinates. Out of the blue, Herb comes up with some lousy idea. Worse still, he begins to beat it like a dead horse. Your patience is more than tried . . . it's tested. And your first inclination is to pull out your broadsword and chop Herb's head off.

Suppose you do. Herb is not only hurt by the fact that his idea had a flat tire, but he's wounded by the fact that you've punctured his psyche. He stops his pursuit of the idea.

Now consider the consequences—to him and to you. Herb will not soon again offer any ideas to you; he figures that if he opens his mouth, his foot will be shoved in it. The others will get the same idea. So any thought you had of building a participative management style goes out the window. And count on one more: People will rally to Herb, because he's "one of our own."

Handle it differently, and see the consequences. Rather than jump all over Herb's idea and Herb, suggest that the two of you spend some time on it after the meeting rather than now: "Herb, I share your enthusiasm, but I think we'd better explore this further when we can have the time to really get into it."

Others in the group will admire your finesse, appreciate the fact that one of their own isn't clobbered publicly, and anticipate that the same fine treatment will be accorded them under similar circumstances. That means they will continue to make contributions to the team effort. As for Herb, he'll probably come into your office saying, "On second thought, I was way off base."

Protecting egos is a way to motivate quietly—and effectively.

○ ○

25

Good Pay, No Stay—How Come?

In one management seminar, I invited participants—all sales managers in retail car dealerships—to identify one problem within the sales force that they wanted to solve above all. I got an immediate response from one individual, echoed by several others: "We pay our salespeople well, but we have a lot of turnover."

I knew where we were headed but asked, "Tell me about how your salespeople work, what they do, your relationship with them." This explanation followed: This was a major metro dealership where salespeople showed and demonstrated cars but were required to turn buyers over to "closers" to finalize the deal.

"Why don't you let salespeople close their own sales?" I asked. "They don't know how, and besides, we've always done it that way," was the response.

The dialogue continued until I suggested that his salespeople probably felt cheated at not finishing the job they started; they did all the dirty work but didn't have the fun of building the final agreement. The response: "That's what they get paid to do. They get good money. We pay bonuses. They work in a nice showroom with attractive products. We treat 'em good." I mentioned the work of Dr. Frederick Herzberg. I avoided mentioning that Herzberg was a college professor; that would have ruled him out as an authority. Our business is different, you know.

I must admit that I didn't get ready agreement on Herzberg's theories. That's because we've been led to believe that pay, job security, working conditions, and so on are things workers want and are motivated by. Not so, says Herzberg. In fact, these often annoy workers. They may be well paid, but know someone who is paid better, or have a nice workplace, but know someone whose workplace is nicer.

Herzberg holds, and experience backs it up, that people work best when their work is interesting and when they are recognized for what they do, are accorded responsibility, and are given real opportunity to grow and advance. The bottom line is that people won't work without pay, but neither will they work just because of it!

The more help that you can give workers, the more you can teach them to work on their own and minimize constant supervision, the more you notice and tell them how well they're doing, the better they will work. Anyone can write a paycheck. It takes a real manager to motivate.

If you believe that money motivates, think again. It's part of what workers expect, but only part of it. Many motivators cost nothing at all, but they're worth a bundle.

○ ○

26

Assignments, Not Errands

Work direction is a basic responsibility of a manager, and subordinates, in even the most sophisticated management environments, accept the fact that the boss has a right to tell them what to do. They also accept the idea that there are times when little grunt-type jobs have to be handled out of one's classification. What's *not* accepted is a seemingly endless string of small, unrewarding tasks that fill up a day's work. That's errand running, and it takes a menial-minded employee to accept that for long.

Behavioral scientists agree—even though they may come at the idea from different directions—that meaningful work is essential to employee motivation. Herzberg says it in his study on satisfiers and dissatisfiers, Maslow says it in his Hierarchy of Needs, McGregor includes it in his Theory X/Theory Y: Give people responsibility, not tasks to perform.

Fundamental to good delegation—assigning work—is a plan— your own plan, or, better, one worked out with worker involvement. The plan should set out goals—what is expected as a result of the effort put forth—and the steps to be taken to achieve the goals. Both you and the individual who will take on the responsibility need to understand and agree on the plan.

If menial tasks are included in the overall assignment, so be it. When workers recognize that tasks are part of the assignment, they do those tasks willingly. Conversely, when workers are given only tasks without the larger, more meaningful responsibility, they work at them grudgingly.

Let's take a simple (though unlikely) example. You manage an operation where, at the end of the day, the place is a mess. You ask Cheryl to empty wastebaskets, Dick to clean the coffee urn, Charlie to sweep the floor, Susan to dust desktops, and Phil to clean ashtrays. To do this, they have to quit their normal work ten minutes early. Nobody likes any of it, so you hire a part-timer to come in at the close of the day and assign him the *responsibility*. He thinks it's neat to do all the things the others didn't like to do. The staff stays at their meaningful work longer, and everyone's happy.

People will run errands, but they work better at assignments.

○ ○ ○ ○ ○ ○ ○ ○ ○ ○ ○ ○ ○ ○ ○ ○ ○ ○ ○ ○

27

Being All You Can Be

At the very peak of Abraham Maslow's Hierarchy of Needs is the label *self-actualization*. Of all the steps in the needs concept, this may be the most difficult to define.

Self-actualization is a process through which an individual realizes his or her real self and works toward expressing that "self" by becoming whatever he or she is capable of becoming. This growth need can be pursued when all the other needs—physical, security, acceptance, and ego—have been satisfied.

Yolanda is a secretary . . . a good one. She's well paid, secure in her job, liked by all, and regularly given recognition for her outstanding performance. Deep down inside, however, Yolanda sees herself as being capable of more than typing and filing and answering the telephone.

There is a position in the department that requires writing and speaking skills for customer contact. Would Yolanda fit into that job? Would she like it? It pays about what she has been making, so it can't be considered a promotion in the sense that it garners more pay or benefits. And it's a job that many people haven't liked at all because of its constant pressure. Yolanda knows all that.

You ask her if she'd like to give it a try, and she jumps at the opportunity. She tells you that she has been taking courses at the local college in the evenings in business writing and human relations.

Jack has been on the order desk for five or six years and is happy as a clam to keep on doing the job he's doing. His self-actualization is already realized. Best of all, he does a good job. If you move him, you'll disturb his life. Each person is different and has to be treated differently.

How about you? Is self-actualization on your agenda? Are you happy where you are, or do you aspire to something different? If the latter, are you doing anything about getting ready? Do those who can make possible the realization of your goals know you are interested in doing so?

Self-actualization—realizing what you're capable of being—is motivation at its very highest.

○ ○

28

Goals and Motivation

Want to be motivated and to motivate others? Try goal setting.

Goals make games fun. If you're a golfer, would you really like the game if there were no flags, yardmarkers, or scorecards? If you're a tennis player, would you enjoy playing if there were no endlines or sidelines?

Goals make business more interesting too. Someone once said, "If you don't know where you're going, any road will get you there." Keeping score is evident in any well-run enterprise. That means goals. Without goals, we fail to see accomplishment. Without a sense of accomplishment, work is a treadmill, and I've never seen an exciting treadmill.

Experts lay down several criteria for effective goals:

1. *They must be challenging.* People have to see goals as something that makes them stretch a little. A goal that says "everything's fine as it is" isn't a goal at all.

2. *They must be achievable.* To set goals that are completely out of reach is to invite failure. Managers who set unrealistic goals and then accept productivity at a lesser level both invite failure and accept it.

3. *They should be measurable.* To tell a worker to "do more" isn't enough. Quantify goals—"ten more" is specific—so they can be measured.

4. *They should have rewards and penalties attached.* Good performance—it meets the goal—should be rewarded both tangibly and/or intangibly. That can mean a bonus or a compliment. Conversely,

there should be a penalty when goals aren't met. Sometimes a penalty can be as simple as the *absence* of a reward.

Work toward goals, and you'll be managing well.

○ ○

29

"Nice Going, Jack"

One of the simplest and most basic motivators is a sincere compliment. When your boss took the time to acknowledge some piece of business you accomplished, didn't that stir you a little? Didn't it make you want to do something else so that you'd get another pat on the back? Of course, it did.

Turn that around. When was the last time *you* complimented one of your employees? If you have to grope for an answer to that question, it's been too long. If you've had nothing to compliment anyone about recently, your problems are deeper than you think.

People in all walks of life and in any business organization seek acceptance and recognition. Managers who contend that the best compliment a person can receive is a paycheck at the end of the week and an invitation to come back to work Monday morning are wrong. Many is the employee who has accepted the check and refused the invitation.

On one occasion, I asked a worker what he thought of the department he worked in. His answer was, "Too many 'no goods' and not nearly enough 'atta boys.'" Ironically, the worker was among the higher paid in the organization.

There are three very simple rules for giving compliments:

1. They must be deserved.
2. They must be job related.
3. They must be specific.

Nancy may be pleased that you laugh at her jokes, but she'll be motivated by the fact that you appreciate the report she researched and wrote. Gary may be glad you noticed his new briefcase, but he'll work with greater enthusiasm if you recognize the outstanding sales record he turned in last month. Give compliments that are deserved and relate to the job, and you'll motivate people.

The more specific the compliment is, the better. Rather than tell Nancy, "Nice report," comment on its data or its layout or its readability. Rather than tell Gary that he had a good month, point out that you noted the big contract with ABC Company. Specific compliments indicate how closely you have observed the achievement and how much you appreciate it.

Rather than wait until something goes wrong so that you can criticize, try complimenting when things go right. Do enough complimenting, and you may not have to criticize at all.

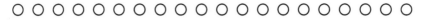

30

Who Says You're Worth More?

I can't recall ever feeling overpaid. Anytime any of my employers chose to sweeten the pot for me, I stood right up like a soldier and took it. And more than once, after being rewarded for my exceptional services, I felt as though it was either not enough or at least a year too late in coming. You have felt that way too.

One contributing factor to that attitude is the fact that most people are granted additional compensation without any thought of the contribution an individual makes to the enterprise. Your company has approved annual salary increases for employees simply because it has a policy of granting annual salary increases.

There may be a top limit or a cutoff date, but more often than not, the average worker doesn't meet up with either. Some get promoted; others leave. In fact, most workers honestly expect annual raises even if they don't honestly deserve them. Even worse, it's common for increases to show up in a paycheck without even a mention of the fact by the manager who is supposed to approve them. After all, doesn't payroll handle such things?

Merit increases do make more of a stir. It's a manager's way of showing how generous he or she is, and it's supposed to get the employee greatly motivated to do more and do better. But in truth it's questionable whether subordinates actually cast you in the role of the philanthropist or that they will really deliver increased or improved services. They, like you and me, feel that what you have given them has already been earned.

Even a routine annual increase should cause some conversation between employee and manager:

- "Ed, you'll find additional money in your paycheck this month. It's the automatic increase we promised you annually during the first two years of service here. What that means is that we feel you've made the kind of progress we expected of you. Congratulations. You've earned it. Let's talk about the future. . . ."
- Ginny, I'm pleased to tell you in advance that you're being given a merit increase next month. You've done very nice work, and we appreciate it. [Explain the raise.] Let's talk about how you plan to earn the next one. . . ."

When giving your employee a raise, how you handle it is every bit as important as how much the raise is.

○ ○

31

Emmys and Oscars

To prove that people seek and enjoy recognition, all you have to do is tune in on the Emmy or Oscar shows. Here are folks, accustomed to applause and well paid for their performances, running up to the stage to claim their prizes. They've won something that is relatively inexpensive. Besides, they've already been paid megabucks to do whatever they do and by winning will pick up even better roles and make bigger money. If money talks, it talks better than those little statues.

But money can't say what those statues can. You can bet that there will be a prominent spot in the winner's home where the symbol will be displayed. The award will still be there when the money is gone, and the winner will be remembered for it even longer than that.

You don't have to go to Hollywood or hobnob with the stars to see similar reactions. All you have to do is visit offices in any business. There you'll see plaques and certificates attesting to the fact that Sally or Sam was recognized for some outstanding feat. Doctors, lawyers, and others use these awards to boost their images in the eyes of clients. So do the people in your organization.

Never grant an award without the individual's having earned it. Bear in mind that there are other ways of earning recognition than by placing first in a contest. Take a tip from the Emmys and Oscars; they are given in a number of categories, spreading the good news and encouraging performance on a broad scale.

Sales organizations are classic examples of situations in which awards can be spread fairly widely. Some sales managers still stick with "Salesperson of the Month [Year]." That's fine, but add still others. Here's where goal setting and motivation come into harmony with one another. How about achievement awards for those who meet sales objectives, or "most improved" plaques even if the participant isn't top dog?

Ralph has the division's best territory and always comes up with Salesperson of the Year. Christine is a newer rep in a territory that requires a lot of digging for not too many sales. Yet despite the penalty of geographic circumstance, Christine keeps hitting quotas, even when they are edged upward month after month. She'll never get the top award unless the situation changes, but she deserves something.

Make awards meaningful. Make people dig to win them. Present them publicly. Then stand back before the crowd runs you over in their enthusiasm for winning the next time around!

○ ○

32

The Art of Winning Over

If you are to be successful as a manager, learn the art of winning people over to a point of view or a course of action. Persuasion falls somewhere between begging and beating and is far preferable to either. It's best when it is applied quietly and accepted thoroughly.

Two elements are important to persuasion: emotion and logic. People who are persuaded must back the urge to do something with reasons for doing so. Or if the reasons are already obvious but the desire isn't present, the persuader must provide a nudge to get things going. People who persuade, then, must wrap logic in good feelings about a desired action.

Becky is in a clerical position in your department. She is bright and talented but not eligible for promotion into supervisory ranks because your company has a phantom and unwritten policy that says people at that level should have a degree. You encourage Becky to finish her degree so that she can take advantage of her potential. Tricky business, this, because you have to get her to commit without making promises of promotion. How pleased you are when Becky tells you that she heeded your counsel and has enrolled in night classes.

Turn that situation around: You want to persuade your boss to let you promote Becky into a supervisory position despite the unwritten policy. You know that this has been bypassed a number of times, but it has been at least temporarily politically unpopular for managers who have done so. Your manager, not you, would have to answer any adverse comment on the subject. You might go about it like this:

1. Ask your manager for a little time for counsel and advice.

2. Tell her about the opening and the sensitivity of the job. This is your real concern: getting the right person on it—and fast—and from inside the shop. You get easy agreement on these points. These are the emotional appeals. Get them up front.

3. You say that you have a person in mind who would take over and do a great job. This person has filled at least part of the job on a temporary basis before, is well accepted by others in the department, and promoting her would meet peer approval. You identify Becky as your best bet. *But . . .*

4. There's this thing about a degree. Your candidate has three years of credit and is finishing her degree. You'd feel comfortable in bypassing the rule—unwritten and previously broken—but would your boss?

You've coupled emotion and logic. You've told your boss that you just need a go-ahead. Odds are good you'll get it. The positives have outweighed the negatives.

Persuasion is bending minds, not twisting arms.

○ ○ ○ ○ ○ ○ ○ ○ ○ ○ ○ ○ ○ ○ ○ ○ ○ ○ ○ ○

33

Scoreboards and High-Fives

Some of the things that are noticeably lacking in the typical business atmosphere are audiences, applause, scoreboards, and high-fives—or, to put it in simple motivational terms, enthusiasm.

Watch any athletic team, amateur or professional, and what you notice most is the effect of accomplishment on spirit and the effect of spirit on accomplishment. When the numbers go up on the scoreboard, players perform with more drive. It also works the other way: When players perform with added zeal, the numbers go up on the scoreboard.

A story is told of the old days in the steel industry when, at the end of the day shift, the foreman took a big chalk and wrote the number "6" on the shop floor. When the night shift came on, they wondered what "6" meant and were told that was the number of production units turned out that day. The following morning, the day shift found the "6" rubbed out and found a "7" chalked in its place. That night, an "8" was chalked on the floor. And so it went. Production improved as the scoreboard challenged it.

One of my former clients was a major food processor with efficient production techniques. As a case was packed, it was put onto a pallet. As a pallet was filled, it was hauled away to the storehouse. I wondered whether it would have been more motivational if the pallets had been left there and removed at the end of the shift. Then those who filled the cases could see what they had accomplished that day.

Almost anything that takes place in a business can be quantified on the scoreboard:

Sales: Units and dollar volume
Manufacturing: Units, scrap, quality
Accounting: Billings
Personnel: Turnover, hirees

Find a measurement, and use it for scorekeeping

Don't forget high-fives, the enthusiastic salute athletes give one another with arms up and hands slapped together. Get your team so involved that when something good happens, they salute one another. And be sure you acknowledge and broadcast your approval.

Change the atmosphere of your department by setting challenges and rewarding achievement. Use a scoreboard, and encourage a few high-fives.

○ ○ ○ ○ ○ ○ ○ ○ ○ ○ ○ ○ ○ ○ ○ ○ ○ ○ ○ ○

34

Maybe Motivation Isn't the Answer

A classic mistake of some managers is believing an employee needs motivation to do a job better when what the employee really needs is help in doing the job. The least glamorous type of motivation is sometimes *training*.

Learn to think of poor performance as resulting from:

| Skill | *Can do* |
| Attitude | *Will do* |

It takes both well-developed skills and healthy attitudes to bring about peak performance. It doesn't make much difference how enthusiastic people are to do the job if they don't know how to do it.

Become a careful observer in order to diagnose skill deficiencies or attitude problems. If you see poor work coming from an individual, watch to see whether the same error is committed repeatedly. If it is, call that problem to the person's attention and ask if he or she knows why the error is being made. "I seem to have trouble with that" confesses need for help. "I'll have to watch that" may be a sign of carelessness brought on by attitude problems.

With new employees, hiring and initial training may be at fault. With older employees, attention and encouragement may be at fault. Sometimes jobs change, and workers are expected to catch on for themselves. New technology in shops and offices presents new demands for training.

Although skill development may not properly classify as motivation, what surrounds training may be motivational:

- Your recognition that an employee's performance isn't up to par shows that you know what's going on.
- Your willingness to help wins an employee's respect.

- Your display of concern rather than placing blame wins an employee's loyalty.

In other parts of this book, we've discussed the importance of workers' liking what they do. Nobody will ever like work they can't do or can't do well. We've also discussed the need for recognition as a motivator; recognition won't come to the person who can't get the job done properly.

The most motivational managers I ever worked for encouraged me to do good work, complimented me when I did it (and corrected me when I didn't), and placed at my disposal the tools I needed. Among those tools were training opportunities to develop a better me. And how I worked for them! And how I loved to work for them!

Help your employees to do their jobs, and you may find you've solved a "motivation" problem.

○ ○

35

Coaching Is a Management Job

There are a lot of things about Jim that you like—and a few things he does that bother you. One is the way he handles his paperwork. He was trained to do it properly but manages to bungle it every time. He needs help. Is it coaching or is it counseling?

Coaching and *counseling* are not synonyms or interchangeable terms. Although some of the same techniques apply, there are two separate objectives involved. We coach to develop skills, and we counsel to develop attitudes—and we don't do them simultaneously. In Jim's case it appears to be lack of skill, so here are some tips on handling coaching as a management tool:

- Determine a need. Something isn't happening just right in Jim's situation. You know what it is.
- Observe an individual's performance long enough to be sure you know what part or parts of the performance could be improved. No question about Jim's errors.
- Ask, don't tell, the individual about how he or she thinks things are going. When you ask Jim, he says he's doing fine but paperwork "isn't his bag."
- If the individual doesn't recognize problems, point them out. Be specific. Don't let Jim off the hook, but show him where he's doing it wrong.
- Compliment the worker on things he or she does well. Jim does part of it well; skip that part in coaching.
- Use prescribed steps in coaching: Tell, show, have the worker try, reteach as necessary. Let the worker try again. Then let the worker do the job alone. After two tries, Jim seems to have it.
- When you are sure the job is being done correctly, compliment the worker on his or her progress. Jim is pleased that he's finally doing it right.
- Work on only one thing at a time. To introduce more merely frustrates the individual: "Can't I do anything right?" Reserve coaching in other areas with Jim until later.
- Check back later to see whether the job is being done to your satisfaction. Be sure to add another supportive compliment or comment. Jim *is* doing it right. Now there's another thing to like about him.

Whenever you coach a subordinate to success, you're assuring success for yourself.

○ ○

36

Counseling Is, Too

The flip side of coaching is counseling. It's aimed at attitudes. Sometimes poor attitudes are reflected in the application of skills.

Rosa is extremely competent, but lately her work has been slipping. In addition, she's becoming curt in her responses, not only to you but to others. In the old days, this called for a trip to the woodshed; today it calls for a sit-down counseling session. The objective is attitude change.

Pete is a good producer. Although he has a lot to learn, he keeps learning. A week ago, Pete had a number of things go wrong, and that's not like him. Through observation, you discover that Pete isn't putting forth the effort that's his trademark. He's sulking, postponing, and doing his work in a haphazard manner. Attitude, once again.

In neither case do you know what's really wrong. How do you proceed?

- Ask. Begin by saying what you've noticed. Then ask why what you've noticed is happening.
- Listen without interrupting. Encourage the employee to give full expression to the situation.
- Don't be judgmental, and prepare for shock. You'll often find that underlying the attitude problem is a personal dilemma.
- Although you are privileged to know in general what's causing the situation, don't indulge your curiosity to the point where you're asking beyond your right to know.
- Don't offer advice. Free advice is worth what it costs. Your role is to help the person think his or her problems through, not supply solutions.

It turns out that Rosa is having a few health problems and is under a doctor's care. Wish her well, and tell her that you'll be understanding. She may not solve her health problems by tomorrow, but you can be sure that by tomorrow she'll act differently.

Pete's problem is quite different—a domestic situation that's going to take some time to straighten out. Tell him that what he has told you will be kept confidential, and keep the promise.

You've made both individuals aware that nonwork problems are affecting their work and offered a supporting shoulder. What remains for you to do is to follow up to see what happens.

Get into the habit of counseling—and not only when things go wrong; also use it to develop and maintain good attitudes. Time spent in counseling will ultimately save you time in correcting.

○ ○ ○ ○ ○ ○ ○ ○ ○ ○ ○ ○ ○ ○ ○ ○ ○ ○ ○ ○

37

How's Your P-Q-Q?

In grade schools they measure IQ. In college they're very interested in SAT scores. Some of the assignments you get and give carry an added PDQ. But how about P-Q-Q—productivity measured in quantitative and qualitative terms?

Think about your evaluations of people under your supervision. It's a safe bet that the weight of most evaluations rests on the quantitative. Why? It's the easier to measure and to defend.

Qualitative is another matter. It means not only how well an employee does assigned work but also a variety of activities that defy measurement. For instance, sales managers are measured quantitatively by the number of units sold and the dollar revenues produced. They may also be measured quantitatively on the turnover of personnel in the department. Now suppose a manager is made part of a study team to advise the advertising manager on promotional needs in the field. That belongs in the qualitative portion of productivity: effort expended, task completed, but no tangible results.

Plant managers are measured quantitatively on such items as units produced, expense control, and worker turnover. They are also measured qualitatively on the durability of the product and the absence of warranty claims. But what about the task force to which a manager is assigned to consider the location of a new plant? This is worthwhile work, but it doesn't show up on any bottom line.

Managers tend to take high-performance people—labeled as such by high numbers—and put them on special assignments. A salesperson may be asked to train a new recruit or be sent to help in another territory on a sensitive presentation. Do we consider the value of that, especially since such activities may rob from the sales he or she might have made in the regular territory?

So it is with workers in any classification. They may be pleased with the recognition that special assignments bring them, but they want to be credited for them as well. Give it to them. (And be sure *your* boss credits you with the valuable qualitative effort you put forth too.)

Anyone can measure quantity. It takes a good manager to see quality. Require both and recognize both, and you'll manage a winning team.

○ ○

38

An Easy Way to Remember What to Do

However committed we may be to being good motivators, often we need a quick reminder of things to do. The mnemonic that follows may not cover all the bases, but it will hit enough of them to help you work effectively with employees. Or, to put it into the proper term, it will help you APPEAL to others:

A sk questions.
P ay compliments.
P rotect egos.
E mphasize benefits.
A ssure people.
L ook and listen for responses.

Ask Questions

You can often tell people a lot by asking a few questions—for instance: "I'm going over your report and am having some trouble understanding it. Am I missing something?" This query may initiate a correction or stimulate an explanation. Or, "You've been on this assignment for two years. Are you comfortable with it?" This may prompt a full discussion of the worker's performance and career objectives. Questions show interest and trigger responses.

Pay Compliments

Be sure they're deserved and specific: "I like the way you handled that project, Miriam. By next year that should save us over \$25,000." She'll be pleased that you're pleased. And you'll find that compliments generate repeat performances of good work.

Protect Egos

Criticize privately, and criticize the work, not the person: "This is the way this should be done," *not*, "You should have done it this way." Folks appreciate efforts to spare them from embarrassment.

Emphasize Benefits

Employees think, "What's in it for me?" Don't let them guess; tell them: "If you meet your sales objective, your bonus will be . . ." "If you can justify the project with a good proposal, you'll get both the budget and manpower you need." Quid pro quo—what you get for what you give—is part of a manager's motivational package. On the street it's called selling!

Assure People

Some people don't do things because they don't dare. Assure employees that you're behind them on tough projects. Make them feel comfortable in coming to you for help. Assurance breeds effort. Effort translates into performance.

Look and Listen for Responses

Make it a practice to pay attention. Listen to what people say, and watch their expressions. Then follow their lead to the next important step in your motivational effort.

* * * *

These reminders may not be all you need to do a complete job of motivation, but they'll get you off to a good start and lead to better things down the line.

○ ○

Part Three

Choosing a Management Style

Management style is not a new idea, but we're talking about it a lot these days. One common expression is *Japanese management style,* an ironic term because Americans taught the Japanese how to do it after World War II. The real difference is that the folks at Toyota and Mitsubishi and Sony and the like listened, and some of us didn't.

We're getting there, though. My own experience has been that progressive American companies were managing in a more open style long before labels were put on any sort of style. But even in the less progressive organizations, some recognized the value of managing by example, by consultation, team building, and organization development, and developed these styles.

Management styles are relatively dependent on the nature of work being done and the people available to do it. Also, there's corporate climate to consider and the consequences of straying too far from what's happening and is approved at the top.

Ideas about management styles and how they work follow. Some help identify participative management, and others play out situations in which that style is applied. You won't read far before you find out what management style I believe works best.

○ ○

39

We're All in This Together

Whether you manage a small work group, an entire department, or a whole company, you must recognize that, regardless of titles or pay grades, you're part of the group and the group is part of you.

How you relate to and interact with employees in your work group defines your management style. Your challenge is to get work done through others. You can do it several ways:

- Exercise absolute control by bossing each individual at each step of the task. *(Directive)*
- Interact closely with members of the group not only in accomplishing tasks but involving them in overall decision making and work assignment. *(Participative)*
- Leave it up to workers to see what has to be done, and let them do it the best way they know how. *(Permissive)*

Let's look at these styles and what they mean to both worker and manager:

- *Directive management* gives you complete control. But workers may resent your constant telling them what to do. And to be in charge, you'll have to be there at all times; otherwise not much will be done. This is the style you might choose if you manage low-skilled workers at routine tasks. Don't try it above that level.

- *Permissive management* is the closest thing to no management at all. It fits poorly in most business situations. Exceptions *might* be scientists in an abstract research establishment or artists in a creative environment. If you're not interested in what gets done, or when, or how, try this.

• *Participative management*—also known as team building, organization development, and management by objectives—involves employees in planning, goal setting, and other work-related issues. It thus raises employees' level of awareness, belonging, and self-worth—all motivational pluses. And because of their involvement, workers know more about the job to be done and the reasons for doing it.

Never relinquish control and always make final decisions, but give employees the opportunity to contribute to those decisions. And value those contributions; workers are close to the job and often have considerable insight regarding how work can be done and the resources needed to do it.

Participative management offers other advantages to you. It frees you to become directive if situations require it and permissive if situations allow it. Involving employees in activities other than their normally assigned work isn't easy but is well worth the effort.

○ ○ ○ ○ ○ ○ ○ ○ ○ ○ ○ ○ ○ ○ ○ ○ ○ ○ ○ ○

40

Let's Hear It for the Team

One accepted technique for involving subordinates is building working teams. Many big companies have in-house consultants who can provide specific help in using this technique, or you might attend seminars to pick up information. Either source will give you direction and encouragement, but beware of getting so involved in the mechanics of it that you think it too difficult to put into your program.

Until you have opportunity to work with experts, here are some practical guidelines:

1. Don't expect every experiment with team building to work every time or equally well. Just as coaches field teams in sports, you never quite know if you'll win or lose.

2. Build teams for specific purposes. If you have a problem to solve that lends itself to group effort, give teams a try.

3. Don't build permanent teams. When you do, you're actually creating a new organization. And don't create teams that will have to function for long periods of time or will require full-time effort for even short periods. The people you assign to teams have other work to do, and that reality should be respected.

4. Because you make temporary assignments and keep teams together for only short periods, pass the leadership role around. This keeps one person from being singled out as superior, and it gives others a chance to shine.

5. When you form the team, explain the assignment fully and the results you have in mind. This may be done first on an individual basis and later on a group basis. Solicit suggestions during your initial setup, but before you cut the team loose to work, have a clear understanding that, let's say, you want a written report covering certain areas of concern and that the report be completed by a given date. You appoint the leader and subsequently deal with that person most often throughout the team effort.

6. For team members, select those people most closely involved with the problem or best informed on the issues with which the team will deal. Also consider introducing someone who is not closely connected but thinks clearly and contributes easily.

Let's say you've been authorized to buy new office machines. The budget is set, but the type and brand are up to you. This is a good exploratory project for a team. Or you've been bothered by holdups in paper flow in your department. A team study? You've received customer complaints about service delays. Can a team uncover the problem? In none of these cases will you cut a team loose to make a final decision or take final action, but you will credit its contribution to your decision and action.

Teams contribute to your thinking; your thinking contributes to team success. By using teams, you broaden involvement and develop competence in your work group.

○ ○

41

Let's *Not* Talk About It

Many managers who use a participative style make a common mistake: They let the inmates run the asylum. Their subordinates get the wrong message; they think they're being asked to take over rather than take part.

Participative management is at its best when it opens the floor to workers at the outset of a problem-solving situation. It seeks input from as wide a base as possible so that an intelligent management decision can be made. It does not seek a decision, but some managers make it seem that way. They're dead wrong.

Subordinates, especially those who have long believed they are the more experienced and more capable within the group, revel in being granted liberty to speak up. What they have yet to learn is that they also have a responsibility to shut up once in a while. Both are equally important if the participative style is to succeed.

Lynn was a young manager much imbued with the idea of participative style. On her staff were two very experienced people, John and May. Their former manager, Gordon, was old school: He made the decisions and made them stick. When John and May heard Lynn solicit their ideas, their first thought was, "See, she doesn't know what she's doing." (This is classic behavior for those first exposed to participative style.)

After a staff meeting one morning, Lynn made a decision that didn't follow John's ideas. His first move was to go to her office to argue his case. She said, simply, "I appreciate your concern, John, but the decision has been made, and that's what is going to happen."

John talked to May, who advised him, "John, you had your chance. Now forget it. If Lynn is wrong, she'll find out sooner or later." But John didn't forget it. At the next meeting, he brought the subject up: "Lynn, let's talk about the new procedure. In my opinion . . ."

Rather than repeat her earlier statement that the matter was closed, Lynn suffered through yet another of John's tedious explanations of his point of view. In the end, Lynn's earlier decision remained intact.

Participants should learn not to ride dead horses. Managers should learn to say, "Let's *not* talk about it."

○ ○ ○ ○ ○ ○ ○ ○ ○ ○ ○ ○ ○ ○ ○ ○ ○ ○ ○ ○

42

Here's What Has to Be Done

Comfortably within the framework of participative management is your prerogative to be specific about what needs to be accomplished. You may assemble a group to brainstorm solutions to problems, but there comes a time when you are expected to make the decision and the assignment.

Experience shows that the more specific the instructions are—"Here's what has to be done"—the more predictable the results are. There should be no question regarding *what* and *when* and *by whom* it gets done. If the question *how* comes into the picture, treat that separately with the individual or individuals involved.

Carefully and completely state end results and a workable deadline: "We have to clear warehouse 2 by next Monday because seven truckloads of new merchandise will be arriving Tuesday. Keep me posted, Jack, about your progress and about any problems that arise." Jack knows that the monkey is on his back and that the job has to be done within a given time.

Consider how much better those instructions are than if you had said, "Figure out a way to make room for new merchandise." You might end up with an open spot here and there, and it's more than likely the shipments will arrive before space is made.

In giving instructions, be sure to:

1. Clarify the purpose for the action.
2. Zero in on a single action rather than leave it open for haphazard choice.
3. Accept the fact that the person assigned to complete the assignment may have a variety of ways to do it and will appreciate some flexibility of method. (And maybe that method will be better than one you might have chosen.)
4. Put a completion date on the action.
5. Request that progress be reported to you on an interim basis. This forestalls lack of performance and keeps you in control.
6. Offer to help if problems arise or if deadlines cannot be met.
7. When the action has been completed satisfactorily and on time, commend the individual responsible for it.

Keep your management style open during the deliberation of any action, but be specific when you state expected results.

○ ○

43

A Welcome Change

Most managers agree that the average worker doesn't welcome changes in an operation. Change, in both our work life and our personal life, is disruptive, uncomfortable, confusing, and threatening—until, that is, the change becomes a new status quo.

A classic case of change often used in management textbooks tells of a clothing manufacturing company that suffered production losses each time a style or a process changed. Output slipped dramatically, workers and supervisors clashed, and employees quit. When a change was proposed, even managers tended to resist.

In an effort to solve the problem, management selected one of the work groups affected as a control: The new style and procedure was handed over to it in the normal manner. Predictably, the resistance ran high and productivity slipped.

The other groups, in contrast, were brought in, a group at a time, to a briefing meeting held by a manager who explained the situation and showed the proposed changes. Then the manager solicited the input of those involved and let the workers modify certain steps. The change, then, became *their* change.

The output of the groups that had participated in the change procedure lagged at the outset but only briefly. When it recovered, it went considerably above what was considered "normal" productivity. Grievances, if any, were minor. None of the involved workers quit. Indeed, intergroup competition soon developed, resulting in even greater productivity.

That case study was done several decades ago. Since then, team building, participative management, organization development, and management by objectives have been widely taught by schools of business. Yet we still struggle with allowing involvement down in the ranks.

Faced with the need for change, never hesitate to go to the people most affected by it. When you make them partners in the problem, they'll make themselves partners in the solution.

○ ○ ○ ○ ○ ○ ○ ○ ○ ○ ○ ○ ○ ○ ○ ○ ○ ○ ○ ○

44

Find the Common Enemy

By their very natures, people align themselves with causes. They find others who believe as they do and form groups. They select among themselves leaders. The better the cause, the more excitement. The better the leader, the greater the unity of the group and its efforts against the common enemy. But without effective leadership, internal bickering develops, and new power structures arise. Rather than fight a common enemy, groups fritter away their time, talent, and energy in fighting one another.

History is full of such cases. Wars have been lost or prolonged because military leaders couldn't agree. Unions have split and weakened their potential for achieving their goals. Religious bodies have split, and their contests against one another have prevented their fulfilling noble causes. The fight within results in loss to the common enemy without.

In your company (or division or department), adversarial relationships may exist between workers and management. The stronger the adversarial sense is, the harder it is to harness the total energies of the organization against a common enemy.

You don't have a common enemy, you say. Not, at least, like the sales department, which goes out day after day to duel with competitors. Aha . . . your common enemy is their common enemy, although not so easily identified. Your department is part of the competitive effort in such things as:

- *Waste*—time, money, manpower, whatever increases the cost of the product makes it harder to sell
- *Quality*—whatever lowers the quality increases buyer resistance and customer complaints
- *Company image*—poor policies and improper corporate behavior ultimately result in diminished customer or community confidence

Step up to address the common enemy and enlist subordinates to the cause, and you'll find that unity results. Good management minimizes the adversarial relationship between "us" and "them." It sets up a proprietary sense in group members and identifies problems that need solving, not just by the boss, but by everyone. That's leadership!

○ ○

45

Get Them Away From the Office

Typically when you try to do some thorough team building and planning, you're frustrated by interruptions: Telephone calls, drop-ins, and other day-to-day obligations that refuse to go away interfere. How about a day away from the office?

Off-site conferences are gaining more and more attention and approval, for good reason: What comes out of an off-site session is generally pretty good (assuming good planning and total cooperation). Do it in the following way:

1. "Can all of you clear your calendars for next week Thursday?" Make sure there are no obstacles before you hire the hall.

2. "The reason I asked that is to invite you all up to Stoney Creek Lodge for a day of budgeting and forecasting." Be sure to tell them what they'll be doing and where they'll be meeting.

3. "Prior to our going up there, I'd like each of you to pull together a list of your needs and your objectives for the coming year." Never waste conference time on incidentals or inadequate preparation on the part of the participants.

4. "Here's what you'll want to have with you for the meeting." Be specific, because if you're not, you may not like what you get.

5. "If you have any questions about your own individual set of problems, I'll be willing to sit down with you prior to your assembling the data." Show a willingness to help in the interest of good preparation.

If your budget allows it, arrange for everyone to go up the night before to allow an early start at a working breakfast. By moving the agenda up a few hours, you might even be able to break early for recreation. Stoney Creek has a great golf course, fine tennis courts, and an Olympic-size pool. Arrange for a luncheon served in the conference room if that will facilitate business and pleasure opportunities. Top the day off with cocktails and dinner. Splurge a little.

You might develop the team effort prior to the off-site session by having others help set the agenda and define plans, both business and recreational. But make it clear that fun-in-the-sun is merely collateral to some hard-nosed business discussion.

By making the off-site business session interesting and pleasant, you'll get preparation, cooperation, and some worthwhile work done.

○ ○ ○ ○ ○ ○ ○ ○ ○ ○ ○ ○ ○ ○ ○ ○ ○ ○ ○ ○

46

The Barnacle Syndrome

"My problem," said the young executive, "is that I have too many people who rely on me too heavily for direction. In fact, rather than help move the work forward, they actually slow it down."

The older manager leaned across the table and told him, "Your problem is barnacles."

Barnacles? Actually, the word is as accurate as it is colorful. A barnacle is a marine growth that attaches itself to the bottom of a ship. It is one of nature's jokes, existing for no apparent or useful purpose. A barnacle gets places only as a result of its being attached to something else that moves. Old sailors know a solution for those barnacles: They scrape the hull and get rid of them!

Unfortunately for many managers, their barnacles are usually long-service people who are protected by tenure and by any number of federal and state laws. You can't just put your organization in dry dock and scrape them off the hull. There are, however, a few ways for you to cope with the barnacle problem:

• Look at your own management style. Are you requiring people to consult with you before doing anything? That's often the real cause of the barnacle syndrome.

• Evaluate individual competence, and remedy shortfalls with special training. Training builds a person's competence and confidence as well.

• Make it clear to individuals that the responsibility they have is coupled with sufficient authority to move on their own. And make it so.

• Rather than make yourself available at all times to work with subordinates on an individual basis, hold staff meetings at which goals are set and achievements are reported. This helps individualize effort and motivate performance.

• Where the barnacle syndrome persists, make the individual aware of his or her inability to make independent decisions and assume responsibility for activity. And aware of the consequences too.

Another thought: Is there any danger of your being labeled a barnacle? Do *you* attach yourself to your boss and rely entirely on him or her for your forward motion? If so, what's going on in the boss's mind at this moment?

Barnacles thrive best under highly directive management. Open your style, develop your workers to encourage them to function without constant direction, and cut them loose to perform. They will!

○ ○

47

Taking a Clean Sheet of Paper

"We'll take a clean sheet of paper into the design of this plant," says the chairman of the board. Substitute for *plant* terms like *program*, *organization*, *product*, or *service*. It's a great line for any occasion and a neat trick if you can pull it off. Most business activities are surrounded by enough naysayers and used-to-do-it thinkers to make clean sheets of paper pretty smudgy before the planning even gets under way.

That's not to say that experience doesn't count. It does, but it also can get in the way of true creativity. Folks thought that Wilbur and Orville Wright should have stayed in the bicycle business rather than fool around with a big kite that wouldn't fly. When Marconi came out with wireless signal transmission, they said it must be some trick. Then came voice transmission—another impossibility to many. And anyone stupid enough to try to send pictures through space should have their heads examined. You know the story.

Long before the expression *a clean sheet of paper* came into the language, an ad executive came up with a system for creativity called brainstorming. The brainstorming technique is simple: Everyone has a chance to offer an idea, and nobody is allowed to criticize another's contribution. Lists of ideas are made, with no holds barred. And frequently what is considered an off-the-wall suggestion becomes the final way to go. The secret is to keep the naysayers out of the picture long enough to get the bright ideas on the table.

I sat in on one such brainstorming session at General Electric Company. It began with the group leader saying, "What can we invent today?" There followed a whole list of desirable items; no idea was thought worthless. We finally settled on one: a device for keeping the rear window of a car frost free. Another round of free-wheeling ideas. One I recall was to mold a fine filament into the glass. It was 1957.

I left the company shortly after that brainstorming session. Whether the rear window defogger came from GE or not, I can't say. But I do know that a decade later, while I was with Chrysler, along came a window with a fine filament molded into it. Brainstorming.

Brainstorming is an old technique, and it still has value. Give it a try; you'll get some good ideas, and some of them will work.

○ ○

48

Managerial Control

Inherent in the list of management responsibilities is the need to be in control. If you've worked under more than two or three managers in your career, you already know the variations in the levels of control and the methods used:

- *Absolute control.* The manager tells you what to do, how to do it, and stands over you until the job is done.
- *Minimal control.* The manager gives you general orders and then walks away and leaves you with the job. He or she may never touch base with you again unless something goes wrong.
- *Systematic control.* The manager has a routine he or she follows in assigning responsibility, letting you know the objective of the job, and setting certain standards for your performance. The manager in this method uses *you* as part of the control mechanism.

Absolute control is annoying to subordinates and results in two people doing the job. Minimal control is similarly annoying; it leaves the subordinate without help and without recognition. The third type, systematic, has elements in it that favor its use.

Systematic control involves mutual goal setting and an assurance of understanding. Both you and your employee know what has to be done and what to expect as a result of these efforts. The completion date, the amount of time it is believed the job will take, and expectations are all negotiated within the goal-setting procedure.

With completion dates set, you establish interim dates on which both of you meet to review progress or progress reports. You are made free to consult at times other than review or report dates if there are issues on which help is required.

The control is handled by the system, and the employee is made part of the system. This provides him or her freedom to pursue the project with the knowledge that there are obligations to meet along the way. You as manager neither dominate nor ignore the employee. This is the kind of control that is beneficial to both of you.

When you delegate work to others, think carefully about which of the three types of managerial controls will lead to the best outcome. My vote has already been cast!

○ ○ ○ ○ ○ ○ ○ ○ ○ ○ ○ ○ ○ ○ ○ ○ ○ ○ ○ ○

49

Setting Performance Standards

Basic to the success of any organization is the achievement of standards. Low standards produce low performances, and low performances generate low profitability. Standards are also the basis of individual performance reviews, and that brings the topic closer to home.

"It's in the job description," says one manager. "If people know what it is they have to do, that's all there is to it." Not so. *What* is not the issue. *How well* is.

As an example, let's take the shipping clerk whose job description states she is to assemble, pack, and ship parts to customers. Cynthia knows that. When she reports to work each morning, there's a stack of orders waiting to be filled and shipped. All day long, orders pile up on the loading dock, and at the end of the day trucks come to haul the shipments away. Cynthia feels she is fulfilling her job requirements.

But the sales department has been receiving complaints from customers: Merchandise is arriving late, damaged, and with items missing. Cynthia has done her job but not well. It's time to discuss performance standards.

You meet with Cynthia and talk to her about the kinds of problems that are appearing. She says that she'll work harder to prevent such complaints. You know that harder isn't enough. You want to set realistic standards to be met. Together, you and Cynthia analyze the complaints, pinpoint sensitive areas, and put together a format by which performance standards can be established, understood, and met.

You list the various functions handled in the shipping room and below each write the statement: "Performance is satisfactory when:" Following that you put quantitative goals to be met. For example:

Performance is satisfactory when:

- Product damages are held at 1 percent or less of all shipments made.
- Shortages in filling orders are held at 2 percent or less of all shipments made. In the event of shortages, formal notice will be made in the package and to sales.

Developing benchmarks for performance sets standards to work toward, creates understanding, and ensures conformance that is more predictable.

○ ○

50

It's Performance Appraisal Time Again

In most well-run companies, the personnel department sends each manager a memo and a pack of performance appraisal forms at a certain time each year. This event is not cause for dancing in the streets; performance appraisals are difficult to write and equally difficult to review with employees. Why? Here are a few reasons:

- You want to be honest, to point out both good and bad qualities, and that requires firsthand knowledge of the individual's work and behavior. This gets sticky if you haven't paid close enough attention to the person.

- The appraisals you write are looked at by your own superiors, approved, and filed in an employee's personnel jacket. This is not something that's strictly between you and the employee or transient in nature.
- What you write on the form must be discussed with the individual. This puts you one-on-one and, in the case of criticism, at risk of argument.
- It takes a lot of time to do a decent job of it.

Be sure of one thing: As a manager, you may very well rise or fall according to how you handle performance appraisals. Do a sloppy job of it, and you'll get sloppy performance from your employees. Do a good job of it, and you'll establish yourself as a manager who's on top of the job. Let's take these issues one by one:

1. *Develop the ability to pinpoint performance pluses or minuses.* This demands familiarity with the employee. Make it a habit to build a card file or notebook to log both good and bad work and/or behavior. This is a discipline to keep in regular contact and a reminder at appraisal time.

2. *Learn to write succinct remarks to support the checkoff items in the appraisal.* Most good forms have provision for both multiple choice and anecdotal remarks. The latter are helpful in your one-on-one review and handy for upper management approval later.

3. *Be sure to discuss everything that's on the form.* Some companies allow employees who are reviewed to see the completed form; others do not. Follow company policy here, but don't gloss over mistakes or fail to acknowledge meritorious performance.

The best way I've found to open the discussion period is to ask employees how *they* might rate their performance in the latest period. This can be very revealing. Often employees will pinpoint things they did or didn't do and zero in on their own ratings. It can be helpful as a springboard for both criticism and compliments.

4. *Take the time you need.* Performance appraisal takes time, and it should. You are dealing with serious business: Careers, raises, promotions, and maybe cause for dismissal may be riding on what you write. If there is any work you should take home with you, this is it.

Write and discuss performance appraisals as though your own career depended on them. Because it might!

○ ○ ○ ○ ○ ○ ○ ○ ○ ○ ○ ○ ○ ○ ○ ○ ○ ○ ○ ○

51

The Odd Couple

If you haven't already run across them, you will: two individuals in your organization who are utterly different in style and habit, each thinking the other is impossible. That's not a problem if they work at opposite ends of the building and never have to interface with one another. But what if they do, and the organization depends on their mutual cooperation?

Andrew is a genius at research. Rachel writes especially well. Rachel sees Andrew as the epitome of male chauvinism. Andrew sees Rachel as a hard-core feminist. Rachel thinks Andrew is a data nut. Andrew thinks Rachel should write fiction.

You have a project that has to be done fast and will get a lot of visibility, and Rachel and Andrew are ideal for it—*if* you can get them to lay down their hostilities and collaborate. The key word here is *symbiosis*, a term from biology that describes the dwelling together of two dissimilar organisms in a mutually beneficial relationship. As manager, you must make it work.

You have two options: (1) Dump the project on them without warning, and let them scratch at each other until it's done, or (2) set the stage individually and form a working team. You choose the second option. Here's how your strategy works:

1. In brief individual meetings, you lay out the job. You indicate the urgency that requires two people doing selected portions of the work. You give opportunity to each to vent feelings about the other.

2. You call the two together. You are the coordinator or team leader. That takes care of who's in charge.

3. Because you are dealing with two talented individuals, you discuss the role each can play in support of one another. Symbiosis—mutual benefit. You solicit their ideas and help them define roles. While you play referee, you look for personality clashes.

4. You suggest that they get together to discuss the overall plan

and report back to you—quickly. Time is important, because they'll get down to business.

   5. At your second meeting, you refine the plan.

   6. With a sense that all is well, you cut them loose.

The job gets done. Each gets credit. Both get credit. What's more, you get the feeling that you now have a team. When you develop a symbiotic relationship, you may feel safe in calling it into being later too.

Teams are like orchestras—instrumentalists playing *together*. Soloists can't toot louder or fiddle faster than the rest of the players. It's the conductor's job to combine and control talents to make good music. Symbiosis.

○ ○

52

Effective Managers Delegate

Management is often defined as getting work done through others. Some managers do that well; some do it poorly or not at all. Why is it that with all the authority vested in them, some managers don't use this valuable tool? Here are a few of the reasons:

   • They feel threatened. What if the subordinate does a better job than they might do?
   • They honestly don't believe anyone else in the organization can do the job as well as they can do it.
   • They enjoy doing some of the tasks. Why share the fun (or credit) with others?

- They think they can do it faster than it would take to teach someone else how to do it.

Let's take on each of those tigers:

- *You feel threatened.* Forget this one. You are judged on what subordinates do as well as on what you do alone. The more you try to hide your own inadequacies, the faster they'll be discovered. Delegate, give credit, and enjoy being a manager.
- *Your subordinates can't perform jobs you want to delegate.* You've failed to train them properly. When they can't do something, it isn't any more their fault than it is yours.
- *You enjoy doing certain things.* That's nice but may not be getting the job done. Sales managers who persist in doing a lot of selling aren't managing their salespeople to do their jobs properly.
- *You can do it faster than you could instruct someone else to do it.* That's fine—the first time. But what happens if the task is repeated? Teach once; delegate often. Never teach, and you'll always do it yourself.

One more caution: Some managers delegate only the dirty and unrewarding tasks. That amounts to having people run errands for you. Instead cut them loose on important projects that not only test their mettle but also give them the feeling of accomplishment for having done the job well.

When you share the work, you also share the fun. Equally important, you get more done.

○ ○ ○ ○ ○ ○ ○ ○ ○ ○ ○ ○ ○ ○ ○ ○ ○ ○ ○

53

Put Synergy to Work for You

Synergy is the effect of combining elements and forces, or, more simply, the whole is greater than the sum of its parts. The idea of synergy is most commonly applied in the laboratory, but it has real use in management. That's why managers are reaping rich rewards by turning to team management. When people work together, more gets done.

A good example of synergy—teamwork—is a football team. Knute Rockne, the legendary coach at Notre Dame, used to explain that every play was designed to score a touchdown. Then along came a defense coordinator who explained that every setup he designed was aimed at preventing touchdowns from happening.

In football, quarterbacks may be exceptional passers and hand-off specialists, but if the linemen don't keep the defenders from coming through, quarterbacks aren't worth much. A missed block or a misdirected play pattern spells defeat. Only perfectly executed plays make yardage and score points.

Most business organizations have people who are assigned to relatively individual jobs. They can't be expected to know at all times what others are doing, but the more they see how their own jobs affect the work of others, the more teamwork will result. Whether you manage an assembly operation or an accounting group or a sales force, applying synergistic principles will pay off handsomely.

If you're interested in introducing a new procedure, bring all the affected people together. Let them bounce ideas off one another and suggest ways in which their job could be made simpler or more effective if someone else's work was done differently. You could run into a few problems at first, but ultimately you'll come up with a better procedure than if you'd done it by yourself. You'll reap the benefits of synergy.

○ ○ ○ ○ ○ ○ ○ ○ ○ ○ ○ ○ ○ ○ ○ ○ ○ ○ ○ ○

54

Developing Competence

If it isn't in your job description, it should be:

To develop competence in all personnel under your supervision.

We all know that the higher the level of competence in any work force, the greater is its potential for productivity and quality. Since managerial performance is measured by those two factors, it stands to reason that managers should want to keep developing their personnel.

People can learn to do their jobs, and do them better, in a number of ways: by watching someone else do it, by being given an instruction manual, by being formally trained and later carefully coached. These are all valid ways of developing competence.

Take the time to analyze training needs within your work group:

- What is it that Jerry is supposed to be able to do that he can't do or doesn't do well?
- Can Dorothy's particular skills contribute to the effectiveness of the entire organization?
- Are there tasks I am performing that I could delegate to Polly if she knew how to do them?

Always ask yourself these questions, and then apply this simple formula to determine training needs:

Desired Performance − Current Ability = Training Need

To use this formula, you need to know specifically what performance standards should be and have a good measurement of the ability of your subordinates.

Once you have identified your developmental needs, you come to another list of questions:

- What resources—people, money, facilities—are available to do the training?
- When is the best time to do it, considering loss of productivity during the training period?
- Is this something that someone else can do, or is it my role to take on the training?
- Will there be opportunity for the person who has received the training to apply these new skills in a meaningful manner?

Take a hard look at the people you lead. Would they be more productive members of your work group if they knew more and could do more?

55

Role Models? Pick One That Fits

We tend to be imitators—sometimes consciously and sometimes subliminally. In both cases, ultimately we have to recognize who it is we're imitating, because we may be trying to be someone we can't copy whole cloth. And trying to do so may result in problems for us, even if our role model is successful and widely admired.

There are two "fits" that have to be considered. Ask yourself:

1. Do I have the status, talent, and temperament to pull off this act of imitation?
2. Would the type of behavior I'm imitating be acceptable in the environment in which I'm trying to function?

Status

Mr. Big can get away with a lot of things his subordinates can't. That doesn't excuse him; it simply explains him as someone quite different from others lower on the totem pole. If Mr. Big is your role model, pick out only those characteristics of his performance that don't rely on the power of position.

Talent

Ms. Perfect stands before a group and makes her presentations without a note in sight. Facts and figures flow from her tongue. In Q&A sessions, she's great with responses. You, on the other hand, work from a well-prepared script and shun any off-the-cuff discussions. She has a talent few possess. However much you admire her, don't try to emulate her performance until you've developed the talent to do so.

Temperament

Each of us is built with certain physiological and psychological attributes that make role modeling at opposite poles difficult, if not impossible. Before you try to copy another's style, be sure you can handle the physical and emotional strains that style may put on you.

Climate

At Super Company people work in shirtsleeves and make a lot of noise. Their language wouldn't go over big at a church picnic. A desk at Super Company looks like fallout from Mount Saint Helens. Across the street at Moneybags, Inc., the office environment is neat, quiet, polite, and reserved. One day someone dropped a box of paper clips, and it was the talk of the office for weeks afterward. If you must pick a role model, be sure the one you pick will wash in the environment in which you must exist.

* * * *

Remember, too, that often our idols have feet of clay; they may have characteristics that topple them from their perch. Before you attempt to imitate another's style or demeanor, analyze any weak points you feel he or she has. You may be a bit more reticent to take on the copying routine.

Role models may be fine, and changing behavior for the better is indeed laudable. But be sure of the fit, or you'll have fits of quite another sort.

○ ○

56

Who Really Knows Best?

The confusion that exists about the role of managers and workers in a participative management environment may be cleared up with the answer to the question, "Who *really* knows best?"

Democracy was never intended for the orderly operation of a business. Recognize that while authority rests in your bailiwick, wisdom may indeed be widespread. There are people down in your organization who know a great deal more about their particular set of tasks and problems than even their immediate supervisor does. When you combine their wisdom with your wisdom and authority, you'll be able to make a good business judgment, and sound business action will result.

If, as the quality experts contend, quality begins at each point in any process, we are obliged to monitor each of those steps. We hold individuals responsible for what they do on an assembly line, in an accounting office, or in a sales territory. So why not consult with them about the nature of their problems and their opinions concerning the solutions?

Interrogating skills are vital to the participative manager. You need to know the right questions and the right way to ask them. Ask open and nonthreatening questions aimed at the problem, not the person.

Responses to your inquiry are likely to fall into three rough classifications: reasons, excuses, and don't-knows. Get to know the difference. Get to know which people give you which responses. Develop the habit of pursuing conversations long enough to turn the don't-knows and excuses into valuable information. Always thank people for their contributions, but don't promise to act on them unless you are very sure about the action.

When you act on someone's suggestion, tell the person, and give him or her credit for the ideas and opinions. Better still, get the person who makes a suggestion to be party to the action. The whole idea is to spread the interest and involvement as far as possible. When you do that, you'll uncover more and more constructive ideas for the improvement of your organization.

Listen to the voice of the people not as mandate but as guide. The judgment about what action to take, how to take it, and when to take it is still your prerogative as manager. All your subordinates must understand these ground rules when you embark on a participative style.

"What is your opinion?" is music to the ears of most people. When you ask, listen carefully, think, and act, you become the person who really knows best.

○ ○

57

Your Authority as a Manager

Who says you can manage? How much authority do you have as manager? What happens if you expand your authority or don't apply it adequately? These are questions managers seldom ask themselves, but they should be asked. Your management style will have a lot to do with the answers.

There are two limitations on your authority:

1. What the managerial hierarchy bestows on you
2. What employees are willing to accept from you

Managers who can't handle this idea will come off like jugglers who have more balls in the air than they have hands to catch them.

You *do* have the right to direct work and control behavior in your work group. You do have the right to set standards of quality and productivity within the group. You do have the right to discipline and dismiss workers for good cause. When you don't apply appropriate authority, you aren't managing.

You do *not* have freedom to exert authority to the extent that you require illegal or immoral activity or deal with personnel in a disrespectful or demeaning manner. Nor can you place excessive demands of time and effort on employees. In these areas, employees have a right to defy your authority. In short, they will decide if and when duty infringes on rights.

The concept in the Declaration of Independence that those who govern do so by consent of the governed carries over into the workplace in a very real way, but never mistake the business arena as a democracy in which votes are taken and consensus is followed. Instead, maintain your responsibilities and rights in good balance.

We don't often see rebellions in offices or plants. Resistance to authority comes off as foot dragging, absenteeism, disregard for quality, improper care of tools and equipment, and bad attitudes. The closer managers get to implementing a participative management style, the less of this they'll see. You have the authority to begin immediately.

○ ○

58

Daring to Fail

We have developed a penchant for security. But that isn't the spirit that got our forebears from colony to nation or from cottage industry to giant corporation. If the westward movement had depended on some of the managers I've known, we'd have gotten all the way from Boston, Philadelphia, and New York to somewhere east of Buffalo.

Progress is inextricably linked with risk. That means daring to fail as well as aspiring to win. We can argue that the old-time risk takers were entrepreneurs with everything to gain and not a whole lot to lose. We can argue that modern business organizations have no place for maverick thinkers. We can argue that, but we can't prove it.

There are departments in most businesses that are stagnant because their managers are loath to introduce new thoughts or are deaf to any brought to them by subordinates. New ideas are threatening, they might not work, and rocking the boat throws deadly fear into many managers. When departments stagnate, though, so do companies.

If you have an idea that will result in a new product or service, will streamline an organization, will shorten lag time, will increase productivity and the bottom line, offer it to the top floor. And if someone comes to you with revolutionary thinking, listen and at least try it on for size. Heed these two rules of creativity:

1. Envision the idea's potential, not its pitfalls. Ask, "If we did this, what benefits would we derive?" not, "If we did this, what would it cost, and how would we do it?"
2. Point out the advantages. Then answer the resistance.

Certainly, it's foolish not to listen to naysayers; they may have good reason to throw cold water on your ideas. If they cut you loose with the admonition, "You can give it a try, but you're on your own," take the challenge and run with it. The "give it a try" is all you need to get going.

When your subordinates come to you with an idea, make them justify the action they want to take. Explore the plusses and the minuses with them. Determine whether they have the ability to experiment without blowing the place up. And do them a favor if you give even grudging approval: Tell them that you're behind them, win or lose. By freeing them to try without fear of failure, you have given them even more reason to succeed.

The more open your management style, the more creative your operation. The more you refine that style and use it wisely, the lower your risk of failure.

○ ○

Part Four

Communications: A Management Tool

Managers can do a lot of right things and do them right and *still* not succeed if they can't, or won't, communicate. Communications is the tool that holds organizations together, makes them function smoothly, and earns their managers raises, promotions, bonuses, and blue ribbons. It's worth developing as both a philosophy and a skill.

Communications deals with employees' right to know what's going on and how what's happening affects them in their work and personal lives. It deals with management's willingness to share information and translate that sharing into productive effort. Enlightened managers have become more and more willing to include employees in the information loop because they see the value in it. Communications is unquestionably the cornerstone of participative management.

Not everyone is talented or comfortable in employing communication skills, but everyone can develop enough skill to do a creditable job. Interestingly, some managers who felt incapable of speaking or writing or holding meetings have forced themselves to do so—and have come up winners. You never know until you try.

The following pieces deal with communications as a point of view and as skills to be developed. They should encourage you to do more communicating and to refine your skills so that you become both effective and comfortable in using them.

○ ○ ○ ○ ○ ○ ○ ○ ○ ○ ○ ○ ○ ○ ○ ○ ○ ○ ○ ○

59

The Mushroom Farm

A middle manager once remarked to me that his company was like a mushroom farm: "They keep us in the dark and cover us with lots of manure." I know I wouldn't want to work there. Would you?

Communications within a business has always been important. In some companies, complete departments have been created to handle the process. Unfortunately, formalizing the flow of information has led some managers to believe that they no longer have a communications responsibility at all.

I recall one company whose director of communications won the "Communicator of the Year" award from a national organization for his excellence in producing house organs and other forms of employee information. A year later, in a budget cutback, the poor guy was out on the street. Back to mushroom farming!

Workers at all levels rely on their immediate supervisors for the best and most complete information. Formal programs and publications can augment that personal touch but cannot supplant it. The closer to the work force and the closer to the problem you can get, the better manager you'll be. It will be good for those who report to you and to you as well.

Employees should know as soon as possible what affects their jobs and their futures. They should know of changes in the organization as quickly as those changes are certain. If sales are down, they might better learn it from you than from the newspaper. If layoffs are in the cards, they should know whether they are affected by or excluded from the action.

The navy expression *scuttlebutt* comes from the old sailing days when fresh drinking water was available in a keg on deck. Thirsty sailors would go to the scuttlebutt to quench their thirst and also to engage in some juicy rumors that were afloat. In modern office buildings, there are water fountains, coffee bars, and restrooms where rumors begin. To stop them dead in their tracks, effective managers beat rumors to the punch.

One of the compliments you can have is when an employee comes in and asks you if a rumor is true. "If I hear it from you, I know it's so" tells you that you have earned a reputation as a good communicator.

○ ○

60

Who Cares?

Have you ever worked in an organization where your manager didn't seem to know what you were doing? You were on the job every day; the boss saw you from time to time; you were called into meetings when instructions were given. But no feedback was ever solicited from you. Didn't you get the feeling that it didn't make much difference whether you functioned well?

One of the landmark cases in behavioral science was that known as the Hawthorne studies. A group of researchers wanted to find out whether environmental factors had any influence on productivity. They went to a plant, selected two identical workrooms, made improvements in one, and used the other as a control group.

In the one room, they improved lighting. Productivity increased. They improved other work factors, and productivity increased again. But what was perplexing to the researchers was that productivity also increased in the room in which no improvements were made.

When they interviewed the workers in the control group, they discovered a valuable bit of information: "We worked harder because it was the first time in a long time that anyone paid any attention to what we were accomplishing," reported the workers.

Say you manage a plant, and production figures roll past you daily. Do you ever comment favorably to the plant supervisors who were responsible for the production? You manage a sales organization, and each Monday you get field reports. Do you acknowledge sales increases or decreases to the salesperson who was responsible for them?

I once managed a large group of traveling instructors. Sometimes we didn't see one another for weeks at a time. I got an uneasy feeling about that, so I launched a biweekly newsletter that listed field meetings and their results. I discovered a genuine interest in the fact that somebody was paying attention to what was being done.

People care. They want others to care about what they are doing. A note, a call, a brief contact in person on a frequent basis are simple ways to motivate others.

○ ○

61

Connecting Workers to Customers

The primary function of any business is to serve a customer. How well that's done sets the mark for revenue and ultimately affects the bottom line. But some managers have difficulty focusing on the customer; they say, "I'm so far removed from the marketplace that I leave all that up to the sales department." It's an easy conclusion to reach but a wrong one.

I used to do a short session on communications at a meeting in which there were no salespeople. The meeting leader always kicked off the session with a series of questions: "Anyone here from engineering? Anyone from purchasing? Anyone from finance? Anyone from manufacturing?" Hands went up in response to each question. Then, "Anyone from sales?" Not a ripple.

The leader then went on to say, "*Everyone* here is in sales. Whatever you do in this company reflects positively or negatively on sales.

The parts you purchase, the invoices you process, the designs you create, and the care with which you build the product affect sales. And don't you forget it!"

No sales organization can successfully move a product that's unattractive, lacks quality, or is overpriced. No salesperson can successfully hold a customer who doesn't get adequate service. There's a fine thread that runs from every employee and every department to the customer. But unless that idea is communicated clearly, strongly, and often, employees lose sight of it.

Consider the purchasing department that, in its effort to hold down material costs, pushes suppliers to marginal quality. Consider the manufacturing operation that, in its drive for record output, lets shoddy products go out the back door. Consider the financial group that, in its zeal for bottom line, sets policies that sends customers packing.

Your responsibility is to make it clear to all your subordinates that what is done in your department has a direct relationship to sales and profits. When workers sense that they are working for the customer—the guy who really keeps them working and pays their wages—they think differently about what they're doing.

○ ○

62

Written Policies: First or Last Resort?

There are two schools of thought on written policies in a business organization:

1. Rules and regulations get in the way of creativity and inter-personal harmony. This school sees drawing lines as a last resort.

    2. Policies, once stated, put an end to a lot of bickering and re-
       minding.

The latter more nearly matches the typical business practice.

Behavioral scientists contend that employees dislike policies just as they dislike constant reminders from a manager on what they can and cannot do. Are there essential differences in these two dislikes? I contend that there are and that policies, written and distributed, may very well be the more comfortable *first* resort.

Policies generally deal with such matters as employee work conditions and behavior on the job. Hours of operation, dress codes—if any—holiday observances, sick time, and all the other specifics are written into policy manuals. So too are prohibitions, such as drinking, smoking, and so forth, on the job or on company property. If these are important to the well-being of the company and its employees, what's wrong with having them published and distributed to all concerned?

Union shops publish contracts, and everyone knows that provisions in the contract are statements of agreed policy between management and union. Some companies that never bothered to write policy manuals have actually benefited from the publication of a contract; it gets them on record with their positions.

The advantage of a written policy to you is that it eliminates or minimizes the annoying day-to-day reminding of employees of what they may or may not do or how they must behave on the job. And since the policy is written, employees who take umbrage at restrictions can take out their resentment on a piece of paper rather than on you. The information communicated is the same, but the method of delivery is different.

Policies should be communicated to employees at the time of hiring or during a period of orientation to get the restrictive material out of the way at the outset. Any policy changes should be published and discussed with employees at the time of the change. Then, only when a policy matter isn't followed by an employee is there any reason to bring it up again.

Policies are marks of a smoothly functioning business unit. The administration and enforcement of those policies are marks of a well-organized and disciplined manager. Communicate the policies and you'll have a well-organized and disciplined work force.

○ ○ ○ ○ ○ ○ ○ ○ ○ ○ ○ ○ ○ ○ ○ ○ ○ ○ ○

63

Why Don't They Think Like Me?

He didn't say it *exactly* that way, but that's what my friend meant. What he said was more like, "I can't seem to get people in my company to put forth all the skill, care, and effort they should. I pay them well, but if I didn't keep tabs on things, a lot wouldn't get done or done properly."

Sorry, friend, but that's what management is all about. And the reason your subordinates don't think the way you do is that they aren't you. They see their stake in your business as something quite different from your stake in it. Many of them have built-in suspicions and resentments against bosses and companies in general. Some were brought up in homes where they learned antagonism, and some simply learned it on the job. Maybe they learned it in your company.

All workers are stakeholders. They may not be shareholders, but they are nonetheless holders of stakes in the success or failure of the business. Like the owners or investors, they depend on the company's success for their own success. If they don't know this, it's management's fault for not getting the message across. That's true in a small company or in a department within a large corporation; big companies are little more than small enterprises under a single umbrella.

The real question in management is not, "Why don't they do what I want them to do?" but "What should I do to get people going in the right direction?" Management is the activator of performance and attitudes that result in positive results. Here's what you can do in this area:

- Keep subordinates informed about what's happening in the company. Make them feel that it is their company too.
- Establish standards of performance that meet needs and are attainable. Let your employees help set standards.

- Identify and reward outstanding performances. Promote from within. Show people that work earns more than the paycheck . . . and that good work is appreciated.
- Never act benevolent in granting awards or benefits.
- Solicit and respond to feedback. Get to know people.

These guidelines will go a long way toward getting subordinates going your way.

○ ○

64

Careful! Someone's Watching

Electronic monitoring of employees is a controversial issue. The capability of keeping eyes and ears on employee activity has made possible not only surveillance of productivity but also of personal behavior.

With the new technology, employers can measure output on word processors, telemarketing calls, receptionist and service calls, data entries, claims, and so forth. Do employees make personal calls on company time? Long distance, to boot? Do they take undue or excessive breaks? Are customers being treated the way you want them treated? These are all valid questions that need answers. How should you go about gathering the information?

Do employees resent and resist electronic monitoring? Indeed they do. And if the issue becomes even more heated than it is, we can be sure we'll hear further from unions and rights groups. There is, however, an important consideration to make before introducing this technology in your business: explaining what is going to be done and why. Communications.

New technology has always caused problems. Take the lowly

cash register as an example. When cash registers were first introduced in retail stores, employees were incensed; they felt as though
their honesty was in question. Of course, that was part of it, but so,
too, was the idea of keeping accurate sales records, security against
outside theft, and the protection it gave to thoroughly honest employees. The company that introduced cash registers to the world met
with such resistance that it hired a communications firm to tell the
story favorably. Once the reasoning was explained, resistance faded.
Today cash registers are not only common but far more sophisticated—electronic monitoring at its best.

Monitoring has saved many companies thousands of dollars in
nonbusiness long-distance calls, time away from the job, and other
forms of stealing. Oddly the honest folks don't care, except when
such oversight threatens personal liberty. That's the line employers
have to be careful to draw.

The story is told of the nail manufacturer who was told by his
accountant that money was being lost each year because workers
were taking nails home in their lunchboxes. To stop this, a security
force was hired to inspect outgoing workers. The cost of inspection
exceeded the cost of the nails, and workers resented the whole idea.
The boss fired the security force and invited workers to help themselves to the nails.

Any new technology or new policy you introduce in your plant
or office is cause for communication. If it's aimed at monitoring behavior, so be it—but *tell* people about it. If it isn't—but looks as if it
is—tell them that, too. The more open you are about what you're
doing and why, the more receptive your work force will be to the
idea. And the more people will help you achieve your goals.

○ ○ ○ ○ ○ ○ ○ ○ ○ ○ ○ ○ ○ ○ ○ ○ ○ ○ ○ ○

65

Cabbages and Kings— And Cake

Two old sayings come to mind when I think of compensation matters and how they are communicated. One is Lewis Carroll's, " 'The Time has come,' the Walrus said, 'To speak of many things . . . of shoes and ships and sealing wax, of cabbages and kings.' " Another is the statement attributed to Marie Antoinette when she was told that the people had no bread to eat. "Let them eat cake" was her reply.

We laugh at these statements, yet they should be etched in our minds whenever we think of employee compensation. Many workers see themselves with scrubby little cabbages when they look at their managers who appear to live like kings. And when told the needs of some workers, some managers shrug their shoulders and think that the peasants should find their own suitable alternative.

I recall working in a major corporation when the CEO was granted salary, bonus, and stock options worth in excess of $2 million—paltry by today's numbers though not at the time. The company had about 200,000 employees. Someone said that the $2 million should be given to the employees, but when that was scribbled out on the back of a lunch bag, it came out to $10 a person. "For ten bucks, I'd rather gripe than have it," said one employee.

Reality gives way to perception: Not how much but to whom; not how much but how fair. Employees who are content with their wages will become quite upset when they learn that someone else is earning more. Compensation is as much communication as it is finance.

The nuts and bolts of salary administration may be the task of another department, but the communication of the salaries and benefits for your subordinates is totally your responsibility. Your best actions are always taken with individuals rather than with groups. Keeping personnel compensation information personal is vital to your success.

Your employees expect you to make more than they do; they recognize that perks go with the title and that you have it and they don't.
But it's not something you want to flaunt, because it will come back
to haunt you. Social reformers would play Robin Hood: Take from the
rich to give to the poor. True business managers pay for skill, care,
and effort—value for value. Pay fair and play fair; that's a start. But
that's only a start; communications count too.

Tell it straight. Never act as though you're doing employees favors or giving away the bank. People earn what you pay, and if they
don't, that's your fault. And if you don't pay what is earned, that's
your fault too. If a raise is across the board, a flat announcement is
enough. If it's for merit, make sure the employee knows why he or
she is being rewarded. Add a compliment, and you've added value to
the dollar. Pay properly. Communicate that way, too!

○ ○

66

Meetings Can Waste or Save Time

We've all been at meetings during which we've thought, "I'm sitting
here when I could be doing something worthwhile." Yet meetings are
often the most efficient way of getting the same story to everyone at
the same time and/or thrashing problems out to a work group's mutual satisfaction.

Leadership is one element that makes a major difference between
a worthwhile and a useless meeting. When a manager calls a meeting
that has been carefully planned, you can bet your socks that time
won't be wasted. "Here's why we've come together," "This is what I
want you to know," "This is what I'd like to have you exchange ideas
on": Those are indications of a meeting that will be led, not an open
forum in which meeting attenders pool their ignorance or are free to
pout in public.

The best meetings are those that deal with one subject. The worst are those that are called about once each year and at which the whole business is worked over. The best meetings are those at which the participants have real purpose in attending; it affects them, or they can make a worthwhile contribution. The poorest are those where half the group sits idle while the others explore some problem unique to them.

Consider the audience and participants when designing a meeting. Will the subject matter be of interest to them, or will a bulletin serve the purpose? Can certain people be invited and instructed to pass the word to others? Either select subject matter around the members or select the members according to the subject matter.

Those who attend a meeting also help determine whether it saves time or wastes it. If invited to a meeting, don't think that that's your invitation to expound at length on your pet project or peeve. If you invite others to your meetings, don't hesitate to cut people off—politely, of course—with, "Let's get together on that after this session, Anne. I'm sure we can work that out."

A well-planned meeting is easier to conduct. A properly conducted meeting is easier to control. Those are the elements that save time instead of wasting it . . . and get things done.

○ ○

67

Meetings: An Ear to the Ground

Many meetings are aimed at disseminating information to employees down the line; effective managers can use these meetings to provide themselves with feedback. The communications process is a two-way street, and meetings are a good vehicle for doing that.

If you were to suggest that attenders should be invited to take an active part in the meeting, you'd find some people shaking their heads; they've been to gripe sessions before. That's the point: Gripe sessions were invented in troubled times when the pent-up feelings of militant workers literally demanded a voice in matters affecting them. If you call a meeting and call it a gripe session, you'll get the kind of trouble you deserve. Instead, follow these guidelines:

- Design the meeting so that announcements can be made early in the agenda. That fulfills one major objective: information giving.
- Pick a topic of general interest on which a variety of opinions can be expressed.
- To avoid a free-for-all, create a plan with carefully honed questions designed to elicit broad involvement.
- Exercise your managerial strength by holding participants to each topic as it comes up.
- Introduce the subject with a combination of seriousness and casualness.
- Never give the impression that you're asking for help in an area that has you stumped.
- Never give the impression that you are going to let the group make your decisions for you or that this is a matter you'll put up to a vote.

Your opener might go like this: "Let's take a few minutes to discuss ways in which you believe this department can cut some operating costs without damaging our overall effectiveness. As you know, our budget for the coming quarter has been lowered considerably. I have a few ideas on it, but I know you do, too. Let's start with . . ."

Your questions might be phrased like this:

"What major purchases can your section postpone without major difficulty?
"What work load adjustments would help you curtail costs?"
"Given an opportunity, what paperwork would you recommend being curtailed at least temporarily?"

By asking specific questions and listening to the responses, you'll get a lot of information. You'll also get a fairly good picture of where your support and troubles lie. This kind of feedback can make meetings valuable.

○ ○

68

Speaking of Business

All managers, at one time or another, face the prospect of giving a speech. It could be a presentation to a small group, a talk to a community group, a convention keynote, or the introduction of a guest speaker. Some relish the opportunity, and others consider it only slightly better than being hit by a truck.

Making a good presentation is the best sort of visibility an aspiring manager can have. That's what makes it such a tough assignment: What if I fail? Here are a few suggestions to help you assure yourself of success:

• *Be yourself.* Forget the hot-dog speakers you've seen at conventions—the motivational speakers who reel off clever stories and captivate an audience with their expert voice control and gestures. Most of these people have about three speeches, all of which sound pretty much alike, and have given the same old stories a hundred times. They are actors, not speakers.

• *Consider your audience first.* What do they want to hear? What will hold their interest? What are they capable of understanding? What can you contribute to their information and well-being? Don't give the same presentation to an engineering society that you would give to a local Rotary or Kiwanis Club.

• *Prepare yourself.* Follow the well-accepted 4-A formula for your outline: Attention, Aim, Argument, Action. It makes little difference what the subject is; the basic plan remains the same. *Attention*: Grab the audience with an interesting or arresting thought. *Aim*: Tell them what you are about to say and why it means something to them. *Argument*: The information you need to get across to fulfill your aim. *Action*: What the audience should do about what you just told them.

• *Practice.* However well planned your presentation may be, it won't come off well unless you give it a few trial runs. Speeches aren't rehearsed sitting in an easy chair; the way to do it is to stand up and speak it aloud. Other members of your household may think you're a bit crazy, but tomorrow's audience will give you a round of applause.

Speaking isn't easy, but when you invest time in the preparation, it will pay off in a good performance. You'll also find that the more you speak before a group, the better and more comfortable you'll be. So take any speaking assignment you can, and make this communication medium work for you.

○ ○

Quick—An Outline

Effective formal communications begin with quiet thought and a scratch pad. Thus begins an orderly flow of ideas and how those ideas mesh with each other for ultimate understanding and approval by an audience. Quick—an outline!

The ability to outline is basic to the ability to write or speak effectively. It saves time and produces a better product. The best analogy of an outline is a skeleton—a body without any meat on it. An outline provides structure; once structure is set, adding substance is relatively simple. Where amateur outliners make their first mistake is in attempting to add that substance as they go.

Outlines should begin with a statement of objective: What am I going to explain or propose in the message that will rise out of the outline? That in place, consider key points—and only key points— needed to fulfill the objective:

Objective: To encourage a new office layout to improve work flow and employee morale
Point 1:   Problems encountered with the existing layout
Point 2:   What a new layout might look like

Point 3: Advantages of such a layout
Point 4: What has to be done and related costs
Point 5: A call to action—let's begin now!

In this key point outline, the specifics have been left out. Rather than try to organize as you go, structure the big picture and form major bins into which specifics can be tossed. Later, rearrange those specifics within their appropriate classification.

One way to do an outline of this type is to take several sheets of paper and write a key point on each one. Then go back to fill in the blanks. This prevents repetition and omission—the classic faults in most presentations.

With a carefully prepared outline, you can write a thoroughly organized draft. Outlining skills save immense amounts of time and frustration in both writing and editing. If your objective is oral presentation, the same holds true: A good outline leads to a good speech.

Most important is what logical, cohesive, and comprehensive presentations do for readers or listeners. They get ideas faster and understand them better. When that happens, the odds of approval rise dramatically. Since the reason we communicate is to inform and persuade others, we achieve two important objectives, plus a third one: credit for being a clear thinker and a competent communicator.

○ ○

70

The Voice of Authority

Some people you know are impressive mainly as a result of voices that make others sit up and take notice. They have, in effect, voices of authority.

There is an essential truth to keep in mind: We are what we're born with. Vocal chords are part of our whole genetic makeup. What we do with them is quite another matter. It's possible to take a weak voice and make it stronger and a shrill voice and make it easier to listen to. In both cases, the voice takes on a more authoritative tone.

Here are a few suggestions that may make your voice—and you—more authoritative:

• *Breathe properly.* Opera singers are taught to use more than the upper parts of their lungs to push air into the vocal chords; they learn to breathe from their diaphragms. More air, more power. In addition to power, you get a fuller vibration in the chords, and thus a different sound, when you breathe properly.

• *Speak more slowly.* If you've ever noticed an excited person speak, you'll have noticed that his or her voice rises in tones as speed increases. Lower tones are better, so slower speech is advisable.

• *Place tones properly.* Many of us fail to let the true sound of our voice come through because we push sound up into our nasal passages. By consciously avoiding this practice, we can improve the tone and eliminate the whininess that is often associated with weakness.

• *Enunciate carefully.* Careful forming of sounds, particularly consonants, makes for better tones. It also helps us slow down delivery.

• *Minimize regional speech patterns as much as possible.* Drawls and twangs are indigenous to various parts of the country. What you'll notice about most managers who sound authoritative is that they move away from these native speech patterns that are most difficult to listen to.

Speak up and speak out. Don't fake an altogether new voice, but use what you have to better advantage. When people listen to you, you're halfway to having them follow your ideas.

○ ○ ○ ○ ○ ○ ○ ○ ○ ○ ○ ○ ○ ○ ○ ○ ○ ○ ○ ○

71

Memos That Get Read

Many companies are doing away with formal interoffice memos. They take too much time for both the sender and the receiver, and they create a need for more clerical help. Nevertheless, there are still times when putting an idea in writing is not only wise but necessary.

You have a proposal backed up with significant data and want to sell this to your boss. Your boss dislikes long meetings, is often away from the office, takes work home, and likes to have time to think about ideas before approving them.

Develop the proposal as a separate piece. Use all the data and relevant arguments, laying them into the proposal in an easy-to-read format. Indent and use subheads and lists where you want specific information to stand out. Keep copy crisp; short sentences beat long, involved ones. For instance:

Market research findings on product X

- Packaging protects product but does not attract buyer.
- Product is packaged in single units but used in pairs.
- Retailers often display product in improper locations.
- Product is considered seasonal but has off-season use.

This treatment gets the idea across and cuts reading time.

A proposal that appears to be easy to read will be read. You don't have to leave anything out; what you do is display it properly. Double-spaced copy is easier to read than single-spaced. Phrases are easier to read than sentences. Paragraphing, even if it makes the overall proposal longer in page count, appears easier to read.

Don't put a proposal in a letter; have it stand separately. Send it with a tip-on note like this:

The attached is submitted for your consideration. When you have reviewed it, can we meet to discuss it further?

Short memos attached to lengthy proposals invite reading. Sending proposals in advance of a meeting allows the reader to prepare for subsequent discussion. Whether the proposal is approved or not, the people upstairs will appreciate the way in which you have communicated it.

○ ○ ○ ○ ○ ○ ○ ○ ○ ○ ○ ○ ○ ○ ○ ○ ○ ○ ○ ○

72

Come Off It . . . Tell It Straight

It is important for us to utilize all available corporate monetary resources prudently and, subsequently, to document such expenditures expeditiously and with consummate perspicuousness so that we neither create undue perplexity nor arouse unwarranted suspicion on the part of those whose responsibility it is to examine, process, and approbate said documentation.

What that *really* means is, "Watch your expenses and submit accurate expense reports quickly so that we don't run into trouble over at accounting." If that's what was meant, why wasn't that said right off the bat? Why? Someone wanted to impress with a "sophisticated" vocabulary.

Unfortunately, people who use such a vocabulary often get just the opposite reaction from others. They're seen as pompous and pretentious—fine for a university classroom, perhaps, or for a dissertation, but not in the day-to-day business world. Worse, when listeners have to ponder the meaning of a word, they tend to miss the message.

Not long ago, I received a letter and résumé from a young woman who wanted to work in the communications field when she graduated from her university. In an effort to impress potential employers, she began with a brief but scholarly dissertation on how important the field of communications was. Shucks, I already knew that. It wasn't until the second paragraph that she got around to saying what should have been said right away: "I need a job."

She said she had *obtained* skills and wanted to *utilize* them to *enhance* her employer's success. I thought, fine, but not with me. I *get* things and *use* them. One might *contribute* to the efforts of my company but *enhance*? In a nutshell, this writer painted herself into a corner by using noncommunicator words to find work as a communicator.

The first basis of language selection is the audience that will read or listen to the presentation. At what level do they understand and appreciate words? The second basis is the demands of the message: Are there terms that more clearly express ideas than others, and are there any technical requirements that must be met? Finally, the ability of the speaker or writer to handle the vocabulary correctly has to be considered.

There are some 800,000 words in the English language. A good dictionary may contain about half that number. The average person uses approximately 60,000—a fairly narrow band in which to work, isn't it?

If you want to show off a mastery of words, learn to tell it straight, so all of us plain folks can get the message.

○ ○

73

Well, You Know What I Mean

It's surprising how often we say things that aren't precise, and then add, "Well, you know what I mean." Of all people, managers shouldn't be guilty of such imprecise use of the language. Managers should be easily understood—no apologies.

Take the word *only* for an example. It's commonly misplaced in sentences. It should be placed with thought given to the word or words it modifies. But ordinarily it's used immediately following the subject of the sentence: "I only wanted . . ." "She only meant . . ." He only needs . . ."

"He only wrote two proposals" means that's all he did—write. "He wrote only two proposals" means he wrote just two—no more, no fewer. "I only love you" means that's all I do or think regarding you. "I love only you" means all others are excluded. Quite a difference in meaning, isn't there?

Another case of imprecise language is in the use of *fewer* and *less*. *Fewer* is properly used when talking about numbers. *Less* is properly used when talking about degree. "We have less people . . ." is wrong. "We have fewer people . . ." is right. "Our system requires less effort" is correct. So is, "Our system will cost less money." "Our system will cost less dollars" is wrong; "fewer dollars" is correct.

Further and *farther* pose problems for some. *Farther* is used with respect to distance: "I drove farther than I wanted to." *Further* is used to indicate degree: "I have a further thought on the matter." *Further* is also used as a verb meaning "to advance": "It will further our cause to . . ."

I sat in a meeting recently and listened to a supposedly educated young man say, "That's anticlimatic." What he meant was *anticlimactic*—something less than expected and essentially unnecessary. Later, in the same group, another man said he would like to tell an antidote. He meant *anecdote*.

Call these thoughts nitpicking if you will, but language use is important to having others understand and respect you. Using the wrong word, mispronouncing words, and sloppy syntax are not marks of a manager on the rise. If you don't know it, look it up. If you don't understand it, don't use it. You know what I mean!

In addition to its effect on understanding, language leaves lasting impressions on readers and listeners. It's a bit like dress, noticed most when it's wrong but subliminally appreciated when it's right. You might call it a class act. Now you *really* know what I mean!

○ ○

74

Time Saver or Time Waster?

The thought probably never crossed Alexander Graham Bell's mind. When he stumbled onto the technology for making the first telephone, it was actually a mistake—he was trying to create a harmonic telegraph!

There are those today who still believe it was a mistake. The telephone on your desk may be the greatest time saver, or it could be the greatest time waster, ever invented. Which of the two it is depends entirely on how you use it.

When compared to the myriad electronic business tools we have at our disposal today, the telephone is the one we take most for granted. Rather than go to someone else's office, we use the telephone. Rather than write a letter, we use the telephone. A great time saver that little invention of Bell!

But the odds are pretty good that it wastes as much time as it saves. When you're in the middle of some serious planning and the telephone rings, you drop the plan and answer the telephone. You take the call—important or unimportant—and return to your planning. How much time does it take you to return to the planning mode after an interruption by the telephone? Experts tell us that it's plenty. Multiply that lost time by the number of calls you take each day, and you have wasted a considerable amount of time.

To use the telephone efficiently, here are some ideas:

- Set aside certain times of the day when you ask your secretary to hold calls—except, of course, those that come from your boss.
- Bunch your outgoing calls so that you don't interrupt periods that should be devoted to handling other work.
- Make quick notes before making calls so that you cover all the business you want to conduct in an orderly manner.

- Keep calls, incoming as well as outgoing, as brief as possible.
  Bear in mind that your call may be causing the other party lost
  time as well.
- Teach your subordinates about telephone courtesy, and discourage frequent calls from them.

In the final analysis, the telephone isn't the problem; we who use
it are. Whenever you make a correct call—one that is brief and orderly—you have saved time for yourself and for the person you
called. If you take time to train others on telephone time saving, you'll
start receiving brief and orderly calls. Then, and only then, will we be
able to see the telephone as a time saver, not a time waster.

○ ○ ○ ○ ○ ○ ○ ○ ○ ○ ○ ○ ○ ○ ○ ○ ○ ○ ○ ○

75

The New Toy on the Desk

Some call it data management. Others call it terminal illness. Whatever it's called, the computer is here to stay, and that's both good and
bad news—good because computers offer us a considerable edge in
speed and accuracy, bad because they are improperly used in some
offices.

If you have a computer terminal on your desk, do you use it, or
do you play with it? Was it put there because you needed it or because
you wanted it? Does it save you time or consume time? Does it replace
an older and more cumbersome method of data retrieval and communications, or do you hang on to the old system as a security
blanket?

Sid manages a nationwide sales organization with forty regional
offices. In the old days, orders were transmitted by mail, so Sid
checked with the order desk morning and afternoon. A weekly sales
report would be compiled to go up to the vice-president of marketing.
Sid had time to plan and consult with individual regional managers

and to get into the field to see for himself what was happening. He had the reputation of being a good communicator and a perceptive manager.

During a business pinch a few years ago, Sid got into the habit of calling each regional office near the end of the day to gather reports on territory sales for that day. He still compiled a weekly report but added daily reports to the marketing department. This gave Sid even less time to get out into the field, and his planning was done a day at a time. Then came the company-wide computer.

Orders were cranked into the computer at each regional office and relayed directly to the home office. Sid now had the advantage of accessing, right at his desk, the order desk and each regional office. He could order a printout daily on sales down to the minute. And Sid did just that. He sat for hours at the keyboard punching codes for the entire system. When he wasn't pulling data in, he was one-finger typing instructions out. Field managers who once felt free to work a territory with reps now stayed at their terminals in order not to miss communications from Sid. What once was a go-get-'em sales force became a data collection agency, and what was once communications by people became communications by hardware—poor trades in any language.

Use and misuse: Both are possible in this marvelous age of electronics. Someone once said that with a computer, a manager wouldn't need a secretary. That's true, because some managers now spend more time doing secretarial work than they do managing. Don't let that happen to you. Use your computer as a tool, not a toy.

○ ○ ○ ○ ○ ○ ○ ○ ○ ○ ○ ○ ○ ○ ○ ○ ○ ○ ○ ○

Part Five

Management Skills and Behavior

In many respects, managers are like chameleons, those little lizards that change color to match their environment. What a manager sets out to do on a given day may result in employing a variety of skills and slipping from one to another with confusing frequency. A staff meeting, for example, may set out to identify and solve problems and end up requiring such skills as negotiating, persuading, planning, and delegating.

As you slip out of one role and into another, it pays to have at least a working knowledge of each skill area. Or, as the chameleon might put it, "Being able to adapt to the jungle is your best bet for saving your hide."

Your performance isn't measured exclusively by skill and knowledge; behavior counts, too. How do you work under fire? Do you manage time well? Can you avoid panics or handle those you can't? How do you appear to your employees and to the brass upstairs? Can you relate to those below, above and across the organization chart? Exceptional skills may fail in the face of poor personal behavior.

Managers often succeed or fail in seemingly insignificant ways. What follows are quick hits on a variety of skills and behaviors—perhaps incomplete in themselves but practical starts for future development. You never know what will come in handy any more than the chameleon knows what color might come up next.

○ ○ ○ ○ ○ ○ ○ ○ ○ ○ ○ ○ ○ ○ ○ ○ ○ ○ ○ ○

76

Band-Aids, Aspirins, or Cures?

"Just take a couple of aspirins and you'll be okay."

"Put a Band-Aid on it, and it'll heal quickly."

The first patient died. The second had a foot amputated. If a doctor gave you such hasty and superficial advice, you'd have him or her in court in a hurry. Yet that same kind of shortsighted action is taken every day in the business world. The trouble is treating the symptom, not the sickness.

Sales are down at XYZ Company. Margo, the sales manager, is sure the problem lies with her sales organization; they're not putting enough effort into their territories. She sends out a memo and whips the troops into action—but sales remain sluggish. Here are some of the other reasons sales might be down:

- Pricing is not competitive.
- The product is obsolete or of poor quality.
- Advertising or sales promotion is inadequate.
- The company has a bad reputation for service in the field.
- The salespeople don't know how to sell the product.

A drop in sales is merely a situation, not in itself a problem. The problem is the cause, and Margo's first mistake was in not exploring causes before she applied cures. Here's where a participative management style would have helped her. Her salespeople might have helped her smoke out the causes.

In problem solving, there are several steps that must be followed:

- *A hard look at the situation.* What are we losing or failing to gain as a result of our present action?
- *A review of possible problems or causes.* What is being done, or not being done, that creates this situation? Is there more than one cause?
- *An evaluation of the problem(s).* Is it a problem? How big a problem is it? Is it the only problem?
- *An analysis of possible solutions.* Is there more than one solution? Does one solution generate another problem? Will a solution solve all or a major portion of the problem? Is one solution simpler or less expensive than another?

That's how problem-solving decisions are made. Rather than take a hasty look at a situation and come up with an equally hasty solution, probe for underlying causes. When you have uncovered the problem, you will know how to plan to change the situation.

○ ○

77

Managing Is Negotiating

Ordinarily we think of negotiating as something only buyers and salespeople do, but managers use negotiation skills daily. They negotiate among themselves as well as with superiors and with subordinates and in a variety of important business practices. The better a manager is at negotiating, the better the business will function and the more successful he or she will be.

Let's say you are assigning an employee to a certain task. One way to do it is to set out the job to be done, lay out the standards, and set a deadline. Another way is to sit down and negotiate such things as how the job will be done and what expectations of quality and time are involved. It might go like this:

You: Ann, we have some problems down in the shipping area that are costing us a lot of customer complaints. I have some ideas about what those problems are, but I think you're even closer to them, and given a chance, you might solve them. Do you agree?

Ann: I know exactly what you mean. Yes, I could solve them, but I'm tied up with the Acme project, and then there's the matter of money and manpower that it will take to turn the thing around down there.

[The manager and the employee are now negotiating. Ann is saying that what she is now doing is more important and that it will take more than ideas to solve the problems.]

You: How long will it take to wrap up the Acme project?

Ann: At least until next week.

You: When next week can you tackle the shipping problem?

Ann: Tuesday at the earliest.

You: Tuesday will be fine. What will you do first down there?

Ann: We should change the whole system—automate some of it."

You: I agree, but until we can do that, are there other steps?

Ann: I can talk to the supervisor. She'll want more people. Can we handle that with budget?

You: Possibly. Don't offer it, but find out what she says. Then we'll discuss it.

By negotiating, you have gotten Ann to commit to a time, accept a responsibility, focus on a single problem and its solution, and get going on it. No orders, no mandates, no stated deadlines—just simple negotiation.

○ ○ ○ ○ ○ ○ ○ ○ ○ ○ ○ ○ ○ ○ ○ ○ ○ ○ ○ ○

78

Selling Your Ideas

Unless your management role is aimed strictly at moving paper and massaging numbers, you're as much a salesperson as the people out in the field pushing your products or services. What you sell are ideas. If you can't sell, those ideas may never see the light of day.

The answer to what makes people buy is simple: "What's in it for me?" That's as true in selling a product on a sales floor as an idea across your boss's desk. It's also true in motivating an employee to carry out an assignment. The standard jargon in the sales business is *benefit selling*.

You want to introduce a new procedure. It is simpler than the current one, it will eventually eliminate personnel, and it requires some equipment, which will pay for itself in a matter of six months or so. The plan requires approval by your manager for two reasons: It will change other well-regarded routines, and it will cost some money. You have the whole plan carefully worked out, so you paddle your way up to the top floor for an appointment with Mr. Big.

"Mr. Big, I have this terrific procedure that works like this. . . . It's state-of-the-art technology. Instead of doing what we've been doing, we follow these simple steps. . . ."

You wait for Mr. Big to pat you on the head for being so bright, but he just sits there and replies, "What we're doing is just fine. Put that idea on file. We'll talk about it later." No sale. Sorry.

The *benefit seller* does it differently: "Mr. Big, we've been looking for ways to simplify our operation and ultimately make it less labor intensive. Here is a procedure that, while it won't produce immediate savings, will pay for itself within the next six months. My estimate of savings for the coming year is. . . ."

Mr. Big is no dummy. He says, "Show me what you have." You have the sale half made. Now all you have to do is support the benefits (what's in it for Mr. Big and the company) with features. You explain the steps, pointing out how simple they are. You detail the introduction of the equipment, showing how its use eliminates another head on the payroll. By the time Mr. Big gets around to asking what all this will cost, he has bought the value of the idea, so costs become relative.

Benefit selling reverses our natural self-centered thought patterns. Instead of focusing on what *you* want to do, you focus on what the *other* person gets if you do it. Sell benefits and you'll benefit, too.

○ ○

29

Third-Party Influence Sells

Did you ever have an idea you thought was right but might be unpopular with your boss? Or with subordinates or peers? Then why not use third-party influence to get the idea across without incurring disfavor?

Advertising people have been doing it for years. Back when smoking wasn't considered unhealthy, tobacco companies had doctors endorse their products. Glamorous women lent their names to cosmetics, and wealthy men gave their favorite booze a pat on the back. Don't buy this because the company says it's good, but because Mrs. Gottrocks or Dr. Longlife or Mr. Wallstreet says so! They call this the "halo effect."

One day, I went to a grocery store to pick up a few items. This was one of a national chain, and I had stopped at such stores before with little difficulty. In this one, however, I couldn't find the items I wanted. Soap was in three different aisles, crackers were in two different parts of the store, and I spent half an hour trying to find just a few items.

I did what any honest person would do: called for the manager. I explained my dilemma. I told him that the layout of his store made no sense at all and that his competitor was not only better organized but considerably busier.

Both statements were true, but it was the second idea that caught his attention. He agreed with me. "If you believe what I've just told you, why don't you make some changes here?" I asked. "I would," he replied, "but people from the main office were the ones who did the layout of this store. I've been here only three months, and I'm not ready to get my résumé updated."

"Tell these moguls from the main office that *customers* say the layout is inconvenient, illogical, not conducive to easy shopping. Tell them that they have declared that they will go across the street, *even though that store is busier*, because they can't find things here." Two things really get to retail managers: customers and the bottom line.

Testimonials. Third-party influence. When you can find an honest way to use this technique, put it at the top of your list.

○ ○

80

Priorities and Panics

"The Acme Proposal was at the top of my to-do list today, and I never got at it." Laments like this are common among managers. Operational emergencies—panics of a sort—get in the way of real progress. Your boss calls an unexpected meeting. Something goes haywire out in the shop. A customer complaint is serious enough to handle immediately. One of your key people is out, and you have to cover for him or her.

These are excuses that pass on occasion, but there are many managers who live in crisis environments. There are a few things such managers have to learn:

- Train enough people to handle elements of jobs other than their own—even yours.
- Give subordinates adequate authority to cover for you on operational problems.
- Take yourself out of the mainstream of daily work so that others

in the organization don't rely on you for advice on an hour-by-hour basis.

- Learn that the much-loved and much-misused open door policy doesn't prevent you from closing your door and having your secretary hold calls.
- Factor qualified subordinates into some of the projects you feel are specifically yours to handle. Initiate a project, set parameters, check on it, and approve it.
- Get an early enough start on most priority activities so that they can tolerate unavoidable interim delays.
- Communicate your priorities and deadlines—even to your boss—so that you'll be excused from certain perfunctory activities.
- Work at home on projects that demand your close attention and cannot be delegated: private reports, performance review, special presentations.

Establish your own priorities; don't let the ordinary events of the day dictate them. Learn to use your employees; don't let your employees use you. Be willing to allow work to be done in a manner unlike the way you might do it yourself as long as the results are entirely satisfactory.

Priorities left unattended because you get too involved in non-priority items soon turn into panics. That's no way to run a business.

○ ○

81

It Has to Be Here Somewhere

Take a quick look at your office. Is everything there in good order? Can you put your hands on what you're looking for immediately? If you can, you beat many of the managers I've ever been exposed to.

Disorganization is endemic in the ranks of busy management people. The reason is that they frequently flit from one thing to another. They're working on a presentation when the telephone rings—an emergency that has to be met right now. They handle the emergency and in the meantime the mail arrives. Eager to see what's in the mail, they leave all the notes on the emergency lying on the desk (along with the presentation draft) and paw through the in-basket. What was in the in-basket doesn't go back there; it too finds a home on the desk. By lunch hour, the desk looks like the aftermath of a tornado. What began as a neat pile is now a disorderly mess.

One simple and inexpensive way to limit paper litter is to get into the habit of working with file folders. If you have a secretary, instruct him or her to deliver the mail in a folder so that you know which is today's mail and which is other material in your in-basket. As you review the mail, get rid of what you can on the first handling. Time experts are in full accord with the "handle-once" technique. And make reviewing the mail an activity unto itself. If you just take a peek with the thought of handling it later, you've already interrupted the project you were working on when the mail came in.

The file folder habit is good for any project you have in the works. Although the contents of that folder may be slightly disorganized by a hurried put-away, at least all relevant material is together. And when file folders get too thick, you know it's time to go through them to get rid of extra copies.

Organized managers work on one thing at a time, although they may have more than one thing to do or more than one thing on their minds. This not only makes the desktop more orderly, but it also gets work done and results in less frenzy and personal wear and tear. Besides, you look better behind an orderly desk . . . and what's wrong with that?

○ ○ ○ ○ ○ ○ ○ ○ ○ ○ ○ ○ ○ ○ ○ ○ ○ ○ ○ ○

82

Predictability

In preparation for some writing, I did an informal survey among some of my management friends on the subject of predictability. I asked, "Do you feel that your subordinates should be able to predict your behavior or your judgment on most business matters?" The answers I got were all over the lot.

A few said, "Not all the time." One said, "I like to make them guess. It's good for them to wait and see before they act. This is my department." Most said, "I assume that they do. It seems to work that way." One said, "I feel that the healthiest state for any business organization is to have a pretty basic sense of how its management feels. Without that, nobody dares move without absolute direction."

In checking further, I discovered that the managers whose attitude favored predictability had the smoothest-running organizations. Those who thought otherwise ran tight ships by being very directive, and it was true that nobody moved unless the boss called the shots.

The most fun about the survey were the war stories I was told. One manager had worked for a sales manager who encouraged reps to operate autonomously. But when they had exercised their own judgment, they were roundly criticized for not checking with him.

Another manager told about working as an account exec in an ad agency. The owner was adamant about how ad contracts should be written—with no adjustment and no negotiation. Account execs who couldn't close on the owner's terms were ridiculed. Then the owner would run out to the client, write the contract on the client's terms, come back, and announce, "I handled that myself." The owner's lack of predictability lost not only clients but account execs as well.

Another manager told of working for a boss who painstakingly made his feelings known. When a situation arose that needed a decision, the boss made the decision. But he was careful to point out to his subordinates why it was made that way. And he would add, "If this sort of thing comes up in the future and I'm not here, feel free to handle it the same way." Predictable.

If you insist on keeping people guessing, give up on any expectations you have that people will work effectively on their own. Forget delegating, because the carpet at the door to your office will be worn out with people coming to you for decisions and instructions. When you're predictable, work in your department will be predictably good.

○ ○

83

Assertiveness Is for You

Assertiveness is often confused with aggressiveness, but they're hardly the same. Assertiveness tends to be quiet. Aggressiveness is on the noisy side. Assertiveness gets you invited to the party. Aggressiveness gets you thrown out on your ear. Assertiveness gathers support for you. Aggressiveness rounds up a lot of enemies.

Aggressive managers walk over anyone in their way. Assertive managers quietly ask people to move—and get others going in the same direction. Assertive managers clearly instruct others on what must be done. Aggressive managers bark orders, threaten, and bully.

"Charlie, this report has to be done by tomorrow morning. Is there any reason why we can't meet that deadline?" says the assertive manager. "Charlie, get this report finished fast. Don't give me any excuses," orders the aggressive manager. There is a difference, you'll agree.

The assertive manager in meeting with his boss says, "Janice, I understand how important this project is for us, but I have to tell you that it can't be done properly in the time you've allotted to it. If I have to take people off other jobs to handle this one, I will, but that means other things get slighted." "Nathan, I'm glad you told me this. Yes, this is important. Let's talk about which other assignments can be postponed in order to handle this on a shorter time frame." Assertiveness on Nathan's part helped bring about understanding and approval . . . and without resentment on Janice's part.

Had Nathan been less assertive, he might have meekly taken on the greater load, missed the deadline, and produced a substandard piece of work. Had he been aggressive, he might have argued with Janice, assumed the assignment with an air of disgust, gone back to his department, and put everyone not only on overtime but on edge.

Assertive managers set goals. They take responsibility. They seek to effect understanding up, down, and across the organization. When they say yes, they mean it, but they aren't afraid to say no. They take charge without stomping all over people. They're open and confident, and that inspires openness and confidence in others. They lead, and that minimizes the need for pushing.

There's often a fine line between assertiveness and aggressiveness. Listen to what you say and how you say it. When you sound a little brassy and pushy and notice resentment as well as resistance in those you deal with, it's time to move away from aggressiveness and toward assertiveness.

○ ○

84

Strategies and Tactics

The higher managers rise in an organization, the more they become involved in strategies and the less in tactics. Unfortunately, some managers don't know the difference between the two.

Organizations frequently promote individuals who have been quite successful at lower levels of supervision to managerial ranks. A line foreman, for example, sees to it that each machine and each operator is functioning properly. The job is entirely tactical: solving problems as they arise, with little concern for long-range planning.

The same is true of a salesperson who rises to district or regional manager. Salespeople may work on a daily plan, district managers on a weekly or monthly plan, and regional managers on a quarterly plan. Move each of those people up one notch, and they get further from tactics and closer to strategy.

Unfortunately, many people can't leave the field or the line. They get locked into daily operations at the expense of long-range planning. When this happens, problems arise; they fail to impress their superiors and drive their subordinates up the wall.

Upper-level managers are delighted when a lower-level manager submits a long-range plan. They like managers who think beyond tomorrow and contribute to the organization's long-range plans. They also know that when a lower-level manager who thinks in this way is handed a corporate plan, he or she knows what to do with it.

Lower-level managers and supervisors who must attend to the tactical aspects of the business appreciate superiors who keep their noses out of day-to-day operations. The plant manager who doesn't inspect machinery and the sales manager who quits selling are on the right track.

Many years ago, I worked with a field sales manager who was a great tactician. When he was promoted into a fairly responsible management position, he buried himself in operations when he should have been designing strategy. He failed and left the company. The last time I heard from him he was a salesman. Now he doesn't have to know the difference.

Although your current job may be largely devoted to the tactical end of the business, understand the strategies involved. That trains you for future responsibility and shows you where the emphasis should be placed in the tactical assignment before you.

○ ○

85

Measuring True Productivity

Marvin has a lot of hustle, but is he productive? Angela has had lots of fine training, but is she productive? This is an important question because we often mistake the appearance of productivity with output itself. It pays any manager to find both quantitative and qualitative proof of productivity. Let me relate two incidents.

Two salesmen in a retail operation: One was always on time and worked very hard. The other routinely came fifteen minutes late and sometimes left early "to make a call on a customer." The manager liked the first salesman and wasn't too fond of the second. Which of the two was the better salesman? At the end of each month, salesman 2 was always 20–25 percent ahead of salesman 1.

A second story: A young management trainee was placed in a foreman job to give him line experience, over the objection of the shop general foreman. The boss had it in for the young man from the word *go,* so one day he stormed into the superintendent's office and said, "I want you to take a look at the kid you made me put on the floor."

They went into the factory. The young trainee, hands in his pockets, was talking to one of the assemblers. On the next line was a veteran foreman running from one workstation to another. "See the difference?" asked the general foreman. "Is the kid's paperwork up to date?" asked the superintendent. It was. "Is his manufacturing objective on target?" It was. "Do the people in the work group like him?" They did.

"Well," said the superintendent, "maybe we ought to have him teach the other guy how to do it!"

Not what one does but what one gets done is the secret to productivity. To be sure, hustle may be part of it, and it's always nice to manage people who are easy to manage. But when you analyze productivity on the part of each of your employees, be sure to consider how much each accomplishes and how good the work is.

○ ○

86

Bottom-Line Myopia

"I'm going to make a profit for this company even if it takes every last penny we've got!" That statement doesn't make sense, but neither do some of the management actions you and I have seen. Some managers look only at the bottom line, and then not too clearly. They should

learn that what puts the numbers there—or what takes them away—
is really more important.

Recently, I pumped gas in my car at a self-serve station. My intention was to stop the pump at exactly ten dollars. But the pump
was a touch faster than I was, and the final count was ten dollars and
one cent. I walked into the station, credit card in hand.

"Got a penny?" asked the guy behind the counter. "Then I can
put an even ten bucks on your card." I grinned a little, reached into
my pocket for a penny, held it up, and said, "Do you really want
this?" I knew, of course, that I owed him the penny but didn't really
think he'd take it.

"Sure I do, mister. That's a big part of my profit these days. If I
gave pennies away every day, I'd never make out."

Bottom-line myopia. Unlike other stations where I had missed
the mark by one cent, this guy was dead serious about getting it.
While I would never ask for the courtesy, I really did expect it. I paid
him the penny.

Is goodwill to one hundred customers worth a dollar? I would
think so. If I were a station operator, I'd rather buy repeat business
than advertise for new customers.

I've seen companies try to cut corners on packaging, only to suffer transportation damage as a result. I've seen money saved on a
product that resulted in losses in sales. I've seen paperwork reduction
policies that resulted in more work to handle routine paper. I've seen
computers put into an office that didn't need them and computers
refused to offices that could put them to good use.

Not every "revenue opportunity" will contribute to overall profitability—nor will every "cost-saving" device improve the bottom
line. Decisions at either end of the profit spectrum should be made
not for the moment but for the long range. Make sure bottom-line
myopia doesn't keep you from seeing the larger picture.

○ ○ ○ ○ ○ ○ ○ ○ ○ ○ ○ ○ ○ ○ ○ ○ ○ ○ ○ ○

87

Problems. Problems! or Problems?

One of the most annoying statements anyone ever made to me was, "It's not a problem. It's an opportunity."

Problems are a pain. But when I face one, I want to know whether it's a real problem, a kind-of problem, or a nonproblem—and I won't face the "opportunity" of solving it until and unless I know which.

Problems come in all shapes and sizes. Nonproblems have a habit of going away by themselves. One afternoon an associate burst into my office with a tale of woe about a rumor he had picked up on the corporate grapevine. "We have to do something about this!" he cried.

I looked at my watch. It was nearly five o'clock, and I had had it. "Let's talk about it first thing in the morning," I said. Maybe I should have been nicer; the poor guy's chin dropped, and he left the office thinking that I was out of my mind not to react quickly to what he had told me. But when he had left, I made a discreet call to someone who might know something about the rumor. "This *might* happen, and it *might not*," I was told. I went home, calculated options, slept on it, and returned to the office the next morning ready to act if necessary.

Shortly after the office opened, I learned that the rumor was without substance. I also learned that some managers had reacted quickly on it and were left hanging in the breeze. In short, it was not a problem, and any "solution" applied to it merely complicated matters.

Managers are paid to solve problems. They're also expected to be able to differentiate between a problem and a rumor or a niggling little annoyance that can be handled without calling a halt to everything else that's going on. Don't ignore problems or put on rose-colored glasses when evaluating them, but exercise cool judgment before acting.

○ ○

88

Squeaking Wheels and All That

Some managers suffer from anonymity. They enjoy doing their jobs as quietly as possible. They never visit their boss's office unless invited. They don't speak up in staff meetings. They never volunteer to take on a special assignment. They keep out of trouble—hitting the quota or staying within budget without any fanfare.

Their opposites wear out the carpet in their managers' offices. They have an opinion on any subject in a meeting and volunteer for anything that gives them extra visibility. They can be found nosing in on other departments and activities for which they have no responsibility. They always know the latest gossip.

Somewhere in between them is a behavior that is good for the company as well as for the individual. The best wisdom on the subject came from a young management trainee for whom I had a counseling responsibility. His supervisor had rated him as mediocre—talented but not assertive. I asked the young man why he thought this had happened.

"I think it's because I do lots of things he doesn't even know I do. I just don't bother to tell him. After all, he has other things on his mind besides me."

"That's true," I agreed, "but because he doesn't see you or hear from you, he thinks you're not doing very much. Bear in mind that it's the squeaking wheel that gets the most grease."

"That's probably so," was his reply, "but when it squeaks too much, it's likely to be taken off the wagon!" I assured him that he wasn't going to squeak that loud!

Be sure that your boss knows what's happening and who's making it happen. Even if you're not asked, write periodic activity reports and submit them topside. From time to time check in so the boss knows you exist. When you make quota or hit the budget, express your pleasure at doing so. Speak up at staff meetings if you have a contribution to make. Involve the boss and get involved with him.

A little squeaking, or a little grease, never hurt anybody!

○ ○

89

And Now . . . the Weather

Wherever you are, you can be sure of one thing that will be readily available to you: a weather forecast. Of course, sometimes the weather people are wrong, so you and I have to observe some conditions on our own. ("Partly cloudy" can result in an awfully wet round of golf if we don't observe a few clouds ourselves.)

So it is with your ability to understand financial information. In addition to the figures that come down from accounting, keep a weather eye open for conditions in your own department and how those data affect the overall operation—or, as is often the case, how overall financial conditions affect your department.

Many managers have not had the benefit of formal training in financial matters. But that doesn't excuse them from needing to be able to read a financial statement and to recognize the important relationships among the various elements that lead to the bottom line.

You can leave the actual accounting to the financial wizards, but you still have to be conversant in terms of return on investment, turnover ratios, working capital, cash flow, and dozens of other terms and concepts. These items are valuable in budgeting and the adherence to sound business practices.

You don't have to have an M.B.A. to know about these things. Self-study courses and evening school learning opportunities are available to anyone willing to take the time to do a little study on the subject. And look at what improved knowledge will do for you. You'll be able to:

- Make better departmental decisions.
- Contribute intelligently in staff meetings.
- Write better budgets and administer them well.
- Impress your superiors.
- Ready yourself for greater responsibilities in the future.

When you are familiar with the elements that contribute to successful bottom lines, you may improve the bottom line in your own career.

○ ○

90

We Are What We Read

Physicians and dietitians tell us that we are what we eat. Undoubtedly true. But we are also what we read.

Francis Bacon (1561–1626) wrote: "Reading maketh a full man, conference a ready man, and writing an exact man." Then he went on to say that whoever reads little had better be pretty clever to make it appear that he knows something he really doesn't.

Modern business requires broad knowledge. Look at the people at the top of major corporations today, and you'll see broad-gauged individuals with knowledge beyond the narrow discipline in which they were educated. The person with a financial degree needs to know something about manufacturing or marketing. The person with the engineering background has to learn about finance and sales. One way to learn is to read.

Some years ago, one of my responsibilities was to assign, counsel, and monitor the performance of young college-trained men and women in a high-level management development program within a corporate structure. These were high-potential candidates for future management positions.

One young man came to me one afternoon and commented that

he really didn't see much sense in taking all the courses in the curriculum. He was a graduate engineer and wasn't too keen on our courses in public speaking, letter writing, personnel administration, and finance. "What do you want to be in this company?" I asked. "An engineer," he responded.

My answer to him was that if he were at all successful in his engineering, he would not be an engineer but a manager of engineers . . . and maybe a whole lot more. He took the entire curriculum.

In that same company, the general manager was an engineer also. But in his rise to his high management role, he read. He knew the business—all of it. And he ran the business very well.

Read beyond your own field—if not for expertise, then at least for awareness. Know what's going on in the wider world. That way you can become the *full* person old Francis Bacon had in mind.

○ ○ ○ ○ ○ ○ ○ ○ ○ ○ ○ ○ ○ ○ ○ ○ ○ ○ ○ ○

91

The Art of Crisis Management

"He knows how to turn a bad situation around in a hurry." "She is at her best when faced with hard deadlines."

Oh, how we admire managers who can take hold and pull us through a crisis. There is something heroic about those who can deliver in the face of adversity. Personally, however, I'm very suspicious when crisis managers perform, because my first question always is, "How did they allow the crisis to develop in the first place?"

Here are some steps to take if you want to be one kind of crisis manager:

- Observe a situation that is worsening and withhold any constructive action.

- Lay plans to handle the crisis if it ever becomes obvious. Keep the plan locked in your desk.
- When it appears that something has to be done, go to your boss and say, "We have a problem, and I know how to handle it."
- Get budget concessions. Nothing loosens the purse strings like panic. Get more than you'll need.
- Put your plan to work. Let everyone see how hard you are working at it. Get everyone in a frenzy. Don't let on that all this could have been done before.
- Write lots of reports so that you get constant credit.

That's really how a lot of heroes are made. They get applause while managers who keep the shop running without a hitch get lost in the shuffle. If you want to get similar, but well-deserved, credit, try this:

- Spot trouble areas early enough so that you can begin constructive action the minute it's needed.
- Make your predictions known upstairs early enough so that when you pull the switch, nobody gets surprised.
- Make plans. Involve others in the planning. Show your plan to those who will be using it.
- Keep a log of what you're doing and when. Cover your actions with memos as needed.
- If the solutions you propose involve dramatic change, communicate those changes up, down, and across the organization. Minimize resistance before you go into the program.
- Keep people informed on progress as you go.

"She's well organized and seldom has her back to the wall." "He keeps things going, and forestalls problems routinely." These, not crisis managers, are the real heroes in successful businesses.

○ ○

92

On the Hiring Line

You need help, and you've been authorized to get it. Your ads have pulled a number of candidates, and you've read résumés until your eyes are bulging out. You've whittled the pile down to about six you'd like to take a further look at, and the appointments have been made.

Before you talk to any applicant, be sure of a few basics so you are ready when John, Jane, Irwin, Kathy, Phil, and Eleanor cross your threshold:

- You've defined the job and written a description of it.
- You've made a complete list of all the items in the job package—the pay and benefits.
- You've set aside enough time for each applicant so that your interviews will be complete and you'll have time between sessions to do some evaluation.

Now consider your interviewing skills. Are they good?

One of the mistakes managers often make in interviewing is not asking the right kind of questions and not listening to the answers they produce. Ask open questions as often as possible—those that produce more than a yes or no answer. Open questions begin with *how, where, when, why, what,* and *who.* They get people talking and revealing more of themselves than closed questions can do.

Closed questions begin with *Did you? Are you? Can you?* and so on. They invite yes or no responses. Questions of this sort are useful in confirming or checking but should not dominate the interview.

Another common mistake is selling the job rather than finding out if the individual is capable of doing it. Describe the job in the simplest and most accurate way; then put the candidate on the stage to perform for you, not the other way around. Even if you believe that you have the right person in front of you, throttle down on the selling and instead invite the candidate back for a second interview.

Exercise all the sensitivities you can to be sure that what you are hearing is the truth and that the person you're interviewing has both character and ability and will fit into the organization.

When you're on the hiring line, you're either setting up a productive future or creating problems you'll have to deal with later. These choices make the argument in favor of careful interviewing extremely strong.

○ ○ ○ ○ ○ ○ ○ ○ ○ ○ ○ ○ ○ ○ ○ ○ ○ ○ ○ ○

93

Do It Now!

There's an old joke about the office that was posted with DO IT NOW! signs. They hadn't been in place more than a day when the bookkeeper made off with the cash box, the vice-president quit to form a competitive company, the general manager eloped with his secretary, and the shop steward shot the line foreman. There are times when DO IT NOW! isn't the greatest advice.

PICK THE RIGHT TIME is perhaps a better slogan. Routine items of business are best done on an immediate basis; the faster that routine matters are attended to, the quicker they're out of the way. That clears the deck for progress and makes it possible to plan and execute important action thoughtfully and carefully.

Time management experts break all actions into four categories:

1. Urgent, not important
2. Important, not urgent
3. Both urgent and important
4. Neither important nor urgent

Every effective manager knows which is which. Unfortunately, many managers don't. To some, everything is urgent, and many items are handled as though the house were on fire. Others postpone even the simplest matters until they become not only past due but overly complicated. Effective managers design routines and delegate them, and they follow up to see that they've been accomplished. They know that it's not wrong to postpone on important matters, but it *is* wrong to let them gather dust. Effective managers have to-do lists that remind them to get things done.

DO IT NOW! is merely a caution to take action on matters that require little thought. A report on what has already happened is simple; a forward plan may take more time. A letter that asks a question may take less time than a letter that answers one. When you get to know the difference, you are not only on your way to having an uncluttered desk but on your way to becoming a manager who is respected, admired, and on the way to bigger and better levels of responsibility.

○ ○

94

No Wonder You Work So Hard

Have you ever had an employee come up to you with pain written all over his face and say to you, "I'm having some real difficulty with that assignment you gave me, and I know you need it in a hurry. . . ." With a sigh of resignation, a charitable heart, and a head that's buried in the sand, you say, "Well, just give it to me and I'll handle it."

Sales reps do that to sales managers: "I'm having a problem with the Super Syndicate account. Maybe you'd better talk to them." Assembly line supervisors do that to plant superintendents: "We have an operator problem over on my line. Maybe you'd like to talk to her." Even vice-presidents do it: "The report you wanted for the upcoming board meeting—I have the data here, but maybe you should put it in your own words."

Some employees are true artists at this technique of reverse delegation, especially when it comes to a difficult assignment or pursuing a department or company policy they don't think will work. Mostly they're old-timers who have carved out a sinecure for themselves and know you'll bail them out. But even the young ones learn fast that the boss will do it if they can't or won't.

Why do managers succumb to such treatment? Here are a few thoughts that may apply:

- Employees are underqualified, poorly trained, or both.
- Picking up on the above, you have established a reputation for believing it's easier to do it than to help or teach someone how to do it.
- You have a sense of pride that's fulfilled when Peter confesses, "You know how, Boss, and I don't."
- Your standards exceed the abilities of anyone else, and subordinates hesitate to do anything on their own.

I used to have subordinates come to me with written reports, and instead of editing them, I'd rewrite them. Wrong. The more I did that, the more work I developed for myself. One day I decided to turn the tables. I sat down with the subordinate, made some suggestions, did a little light blue-penciling, and turned the job back *to the person who should be doing it*. Eventually, most people developed the skills to do the job.

People who *really* need help will and should come to you. But if you manage well, most of your employees can handle assignments on their own. Productivity will increase, and you will do a lot less of someone else's work.

○ ○ ○ ○ ○ ○ ○ ○ ○ ○ ○ ○ ○ ○ ○ ○ ○ ○ ○ ○

95

Stress: We All Meet It

Stress is common in the lives of businessmen and -women. Indeed, when some individuals find themselves without stress, they go out in search of it! How you meet stress is the key issue.

Stress is acknowledged as a contributing factor in some 70 percent of all illnesses. Carmen thought she was particularly susceptible to colds, but then she noticed that whenever she got the sniffles, it was shortly after undergoing stressful periods at work. Jim had an annoying back problem; it, too, emerged following stress at work.

Some people avoid stress; others know how to manage it. If you can't avoid it—and few managers can—it's important to know how to cope with it. Here are a few practical tips on the subject:

* *Manage time better.* Too many managers find themselves at the end of a day without having crossed out a single item on their to-do list. They have allowed the day's events to control them instead of their controlling the events.

* *Leave the office at the office.* Admittedly, this is sometimes difficult to do. If you do lug a briefcase home, restrict its contents to reading matter—no reports to write; that's in-office stuff. Some successful managers schedule home and family time in such a way as to make homework impossible on many evenings.

* *Delegate.* Be sure the person to whom you hand over an assignment knows what to do. Then let that person do it. The job may not be done the way *you* would do it, but it's one less pressure on you.

* *Prioritize.* Focus on the important and pull back on the trivial. It's surprising how much junk clutters the average day.

* *Get a physical checkup.* If you have a health problem, get it cared for. If you haven't, the reassurance will take some pressure off you.

If you try to do too much, too fast you'll be stressed—and work done under stress is usually substandard.

○ ○ ○ ○ ○ ○ ○ ○ ○ ○ ○ ○ ○ ○ ○ ○ ○ ○ ○ ○

96

Good, Bad, and You Got Me Guessing

Take a minute and analyze qualities of managers you've known. Often a single person will have good qualities, bad ones, and guess what?

Will is bright. He is self-confident. He speaks with real authority. We give him high marks for that. But because he's bright, he can't understand why others fail to see what he sees or know what he knows. His self-confidence often turns into arrogance, and sometimes when he's called upon to reexplain his views, he becomes abrasive. At his best, he's marvelous, but when these negatives appear, we don't like Will very much.

Gail knows the business like the back of her hand. She's well educated, has been with the company a long time, and has risen from a lesser role to one in middle management. She's an able communicator too. But Gail is possessive. She won't share information, builds fences around her department, and isn't at all receptive to change. You admire her at times, but can you honestly say you like her?

Mark is creative. He's a good planner and organizer. Some of the major breakthroughs in the company have come out of his department. Quite a guy. But some people who work under Mark resent him, and for good reason. Mark takes credit at times for things people in his department have suggested. He has, on the strength of his early successes, become a risk taker. And when some of his hairbrained ventures fall through, he's not above spreading at least part of the blame on others. You'd like to have Mark working for you, but would you want to work for him?

Nikki has everyone wondering about her. She's efficient yet seems to have time to visit with anyone anytime. She's quick—can throw a project together in a hurry—and is a real clutch player. But in her rush-about way, she has sometimes let details fall through the cracks and has been labeled as somewhere between unreliable and careless. What do you know about Nikki?

Most of us have admirable traits we hope others will spot and admire. If we're wise, we play to those strengths. But all too often, the strengths become weaknesses when overused. Self-confidence is just a step away from arrogance. Patience can grow into complacency. Directness is a cousin to abrasiveness. Sociability may come across as being unbusinesslike. And so on.

Make a list of your good qualities. Next to them, list the bad ones. Does one list cancel the other? And can you see yourself as others might see you? More important, can you change yourself into what you'd like others to see?

○ ○

97

Good Old What's-His-Name

One of the basic steps in learning almost anything is the admission that you don't know how. That's true of swimming, playing tennis or golf—and remembering names. If you share a memory deficiency with me, here's how to overcome it:

• *Be conscious of the need for remembering*. As you walk into someone's office for the first time and are introduced, remind yourself that the most important thing to do *first* is get that person's name. There may be other, more important things on your mind; nevertheless, for the first few seconds, concentrate on the name.

• *Repeat the name upon hearing it*. "My name is Jim Dandy," says the other person. You say, "Nice to meet you, Jim," then, to yourself, "Jim Dandy, Jim Dandy."

- *Use association techniques.* Say to yourself, "Dandy. Fine and dandy . . . isn't that handy?" Or to take a more difficult name like Herkowitz, you might think: "Herk, perk, witz, blitz."

- *Write the name down.* If opportunity presents itself to do it immediately, so much the better. If not, be sure to do it later. You might even ask the other person for the spelling of his or her name, unless it's an easy one like Smith, Jones, or Brown.

- *Use the other person's name in the conversation to reinforce the memory considerably.*

Last week I was waiting for an elevator, and a man who was also waiting came over to me and said, "How are you? I haven't seen you in several years, and maybe you don't remember me. My name is . . ." I then recognized him and returned the kindness with my name. We talked together for several minutes, missing several elevators in the process.

If you can't remember names, do what my friend did: Introduce yourself, and you'll get the other person's name in return!

○ ○ ○ ○ ○ ○ ○ ○ ○ ○ ○ ○ ○ ○ ○ ○ ○ ○ ○ ○

98

Let's Go to Lunch

Going to lunch says something about a manager. Not the mere fact of going to eat, that is, but where, how long, and with whom.

I understand brown baggers. You can save a lot of time, eat precisely what you want, save money, do some reading, make a few telephone calls, and enjoy a little privacy to boot. But managers who brown-bag miss a lot: sociability, new ideas, a change of scenery, and—as the political animals might add—visibility.

I also understand "the club" crowd. It's enjoyable to spin over to the country club or to a fine restaurant with a few peers and maybe a customer. But a lot of subordinates and even peers don't admire a manager whose lunch expands into the afternoon.

I've enjoyed business lunches at private clubs, hotel dining rooms, executive suites, management rooms, and plain old employee cafeterias. I can't really say that much business ever got transacted during any of them. These days more and more companies are going to single in-house eating facilities. With that move, it's relatively safe to say that lunch is no longer a business activity. And that may not be all bad!

You will do well to vary your luncheon habits: an hour with the boss one day, an hour with a peer another, and maybe an informal time with a subordinate from time to time. And what's wrong with slipping out, grabbing a burger, and taking a walk or doing some personal shopping once in a while?

Look at lunchtime as a good time to touch base with a variety of people. Listen, observe, and get a feel for what's in the wind. It's also a good time to change pace and take on mental as well as physical nourishment.

○ ○

29

Did Someone Say "Dress Code"?

There's the old story about the British officer who was apprehended one night clad only in his underwear, following an equally scantily attired lady. He was charged with being out of uniform until his legal counsel found an item in the manual that said that "an officer should be in full uniform except for those occasions in which he was suitably attired for the sport he was engaged in." Dress codes.

An inner-city school recently adopted a dress code "so that differences would not be noted in the financial backgrounds of the pupils." The ruling was obviously made by people who forgot that the requirement meant parents with little money for even the basics had to go out and buy new duds for their kids. Dress codes.

I worked for an agency that did business with a major company in which protocol was king. One day I went to make a call at the great company, only to find I was early for my appointment. Good . . . time to shop for a suit at a nearby store. I looked at the rack and found very conservative suits and asked the clerk whether these were all he had in stock. "Are you with *the company*?" he asked. "No," I replied. So he took me into the back room where outsiders like me might be able to find something. Dress codes.

Jokes aside, appropriate dress makes sense. But it should be a matter of understanding that is set by example, not by mandate. Don't hesitate to bring inappropriate dress to the attention of employees. Cleanliness and neatness should be the first matter of business.

Do employees interface with customers? Does the work being done allow or require certain apparel? Will a higher level of dress work a hardship on the employee? These are the important questions.

Examples tend to be followed. Establish a pattern; then get the word out to a few, and the many will follow. General suggestions work better than specific requests because they are easier to follow and harder to attack.

There's a dress code in your company—if it's not expressed, it's implied. Take your cue from up in the ranks, and that will let you set a defensible example for subordinates to follow.

○ ○ ○ ○ ○ ○ ○ ○ ○ ○ ○ ○ ○ ○ ○ ○ ○ ○ ○ ○

100

Creative Accounting

The expense report has been known by a number of names—*swindle sheet,* for one. Of all the reports managers turn in, the expense report probably takes the most time per sheets of paper involved. It's a little like the IRS's Form 1040; you don't want to make any errors, *and* you don't want to come out with the short straw.

Whether it's your report or reports of others you have to approve, here are a few thoughts that help abbreviate the process and turn the experience into a win-win situation:

• Keep daily running logs. This is true whether the expenses are incurred locally or on the road. You won't overlook minor expenses, and if questions arise about the validity of a given expense, it is relatively easy to explain.

• Submit reports as early after the expense is incurred as is reasonable and in line with company policies and procedures. Prompt reporting does away with errors and simplifies audits.

• If admissible expenses are not prescribed by policy, an *understanding* regarding them should be reached. This understanding should be flexible enough to acknowledge the difference in costs in various parts of the country. A dinner in New York or Chicago may not taste any better than one in East Muleshoe, but it will certainly cost a lot more. Ditto on the tips and local transportation.

• Do away with odd cents if policy approves it. Some travelers believe that when they list an expense at $6.13 or one at $15.96, they are adding a sense of accuracy and validity to the report. But reporting in full or half dollars is sensible and timesaving.

• Discuss expense reports with your boss and your subordinates from time to time. Unusual expenses can and do occur. And it's good practice to let others know you know what's going on.

At issue here are not nickels, dimes, and dollars, but stewardship. Your personal expense reports tell your boss a lot about you. The manner in which you monitor expense reports of employees tells them about you, too. Gain a reputation for integrity, and you'll build a positive image of leadership as well. Honesty, for some, is the highest form of creativity!

○ ○

101

The Leader Within . . . Let It Out!

There are notes of envy *and* cynicism in the idea that those who succeed in management are either lucky, have a sponsor, or haven't truly
been tested on the anvil of life. Yet there may be some truth in that.
We all know people who inherited a business, married the boss's son
or daughter, or were in the right place at the right time.

My point is not to argue either side but to put some perspective
on where *you* are now. The question is, "Are you doing what you
should with what you have?" Or, to put it another way, "Are you
creating some luck for yourself, attracting sponsorship, and getting
to the right place at the right time?" Are you, in other words, using
you properly?

Assuming you haven't been born to the purple, are you capable
of commanding respect as a result of how you dress and handle yourself? Can you speak and write without fear of criticism? If anyone
were to meet you on the street or in your office, would he or she sense
managerial qualities in you?

Do you take assignments and work them through as though you
owned the business? Are your decisions pointed specifically at having
the business succeed rather than serving your own special interests?
Are you demonstrating to someone above you—your sponsor, if you
will—that you are capable of handling more demanding assignments?

And in your relationships downward in the organization, are you
considerate of those who report to and through you? That doesn't
mean coddling people or letting them get by with less than the best
skill, care, and effort, but it does mean helping and guiding them to
good performances. Will they remember you as a manager who con-
tributed to their own progress as well as to your own?

The French expression *noblesse oblige*, the moral obligation of the nobility to conduct themselves honorably and with charity, is basic to managerial success. Not long ago, a former military commander died. He was remembered not for the battles won but that he "looked out for his men."

Admittedly some managers are light-years ahead of others in terms of built-in advantages, but there are many, many more who have made up the difference by what they do and how they think and act. The secret isn't entirely in working hard but largely in working smart. Looking ahead isn't all there is to success; looking around may be equally valuable.

The emphasis today is on leadership. The ancients looked to kings and princes to lead. We're fresh out of kings and princes, so it's up to us ordinary folks to do the job. But take heart—most of the qualities of leadership are within you. What you have to do is let them out!

○ ○

Part Six

Effective Relationships on the Job

Relationships in the workplace have more to do with our success as managers than we like to admit. Talent? Yes. Know-how? Sure. Character? That too. But none of those factors can work to our advantage if we can't get along with others.

Normally we think of interpersonal relationships as important in a manager's influence over subordinates. This is a major consideration, but we must not ignore that relationships up and across must accompany relationships down. You can have your own work group totally on your side—willing to go to the ends of the earth for you—but if you can't get the boss's approval or the cooperation of your peers, you have a problem.

On the surface of all this, we might conclude that being nice and being careful not to cross wires with anyone is all there is to it. Not so. Business relationships are tested daily in situations where disagreement is potentially more common than agreement. And therein lies a challenge: Can you disagree without being disagreeable? Can you gain your point without pulverizing a peer whose point is opposite yours? And what about your boss? Can you handle problems upstairs?

In this section, you'll find a variety of situations in which interpersonal relationships are tested and for which reasonably simple answers are applied. They'll give you an idea or two to put to work in your job.

○ ○ ○ ○ ○ ○ ○ ○ ○ ○ ○ ○ ○ ○ ○ ○ ○ ○ ○ ○

102

Older Workers, Younger Managers

During the Great Depression of the 1930s, Franklin Roosevelt pushed through legislation that resulted in Social Security. Although it was designed to provide some minor and basic support for the elderly, it had an ulterior motive: to move older workers out of the work force and make room for younger ones.

For a long time, 65 was the mandatory retirement age. New legislation frowns on pushing older workers out, so it's not uncommon to have older workers in the work force. That's sometimes a problem for newer managers: They feel awkward giving direction to Old Edgar or Old Matilda. But they're on your payroll; as long as they perform adequately, they're yours to manage. And just as you have reservations about having them, Edgar and Matilda may feel they're stuck with you.

Edgar has been with the company for forty-three years. He started as an office boy and after a variety of positions became foreman of the shipping room. At age 68, Edgar still runs a tight ship, although he's not well and takes a lot of medication.

Matilda is also 68. She came to the company as a file clerk, became a bookkeeper, and still knows more about the financial condition of the company than the owners do. She never misses a day of work, but she resists change. If Matilda had her way, new technology and new ideas would be banished forever. She grumbles, but she finally accepts it.

Learn to forget age and look at performance. Legally, you cannot fire people or treat them differently from others in your organization simply because of their age. Be frank in asking them about any retirement plans; indicate that your concern is not being surprised when they call it quits. You do, after all, have to look forward to replacing them when that happens. What you don't want is to lose Matilda and Edgar only to discover how truly valuable they have been.

One way to motivate older workers is to have them train new hands, or the people you're strongly considering as their replacements. That could lighten their work load and get them thinking about the future. Make very sure you do it with respect and concern.

Businesses need older workers. Their experience, skill, and loyalty are valuable. Like any other employees, they need to feel needed, that they are earning their way and are respected for themselves, not for or in spite of their age. Don't let them exercise any special benefits as a result of age, and don't be surprised if they thank you for treating them like just plain folks.

Your responsibility is to your department for all the help you can give it. Age is immaterial; performance is what counts. If you're a good manager, people of all ages will respect, follow, cooperate, and produce for you.

○ ○

103

Sociability or Friendship?

You'll frequently have to walk the thin line between being sociable or becoming a friend. This applies up, down, and across organizations. Conventional wisdom dictates finding close friends away from the office, even though you may enjoy social contacts with some co-workers.

Case History 1

In a small division of a large corporation, there was a group of individuals in the same department. They had been transferred into a relatively small community at roughly the same time. It was natural that they found comfort in one another and developed a regular Saturday night get-together. They and their wives became known variously as "the group," "the clan," or the "Midvale Mafia."

Eventually business differences spilled over into social affairs. Social irritations spilled into office relationships. One promotion, one dismissal, and one transfer broke up the group. As one member admitted, not a moment too soon.

Case History 2

The guys at the office had a standing date to play golf each Saturday morning. Again, the office came to the first tee, and the nineteenth hole turned into a staff meeting. When the regular golf date was finally broken, things began to smooth out at the office as well.

Case History 3

Pat and Tracy had gone to college together. They began to work at the same company but in different departments. Tracy was the more assertive of the two, and she got a promotion. That meant some noon meetings in the management dining room, and her daily lunches with Pat were less frequent. Although Tracy occasionally asked Pat to lunch away from the office, Pat began to find excuses not to do so. By the time Pat got her promotion into supervision, the friendship had been cooled dramatically.

* * * *

Being sociable is important, but recognize the dangers of building too close alliances with others in the same organization—with peers as well as with subordinates. Enjoy a day on the golf course with fellow workers, but not always. Go out for a drink on Friday evening with the gang, but not always. It's a thin line to walk. Falling off on either side isn't pleasant for anyone.

○ ○

104

Handling Objections

An old cliché says, "Disagree without being disagreeable." There's a way to make that a reality.

Most arguments begin not when two individuals fail to come to a mutual conclusion or a compromise but when one person pursues a point without regard to another person's feelings. When feelings get in the way of facts, something hits the fan. Arguments are objections not well handled. To avoid falling into this trap, follow this highly regarded routine for handling objections:

- Listen. Hear out the other person's point of view.

- Be sure you are dealing with the right objection. Ask, "Am I correct that what you're saying is . . ." Let the other person know that you're on the right target.

- Agree with the other person's right to disagree. Say, "I can see how you feel about that . . ." or, "That's a perfectly understandable position . . ." or, "I have felt that way myself." This does not say you agree, but it does say you aren't about to argue. Many managers say, "Yes, but . . ." and this is too harsh a way to turn the corner.

- Many objections rise out of misunderstandings. If you sense this to be the case, take the blame for not explaining the idea properly. "I'm afraid I didn't make that point clear" is more palatable than, "You didn't understand what I said."

- Restate your own views one step at a time to isolate major and minor areas of disagreement. Perhaps you can negotiate on the more serious ones.

- As you make a point, check with the objector regarding his or her feelings, agreements, or disagreements.

- When you achieve agreement through new understanding and adjustment, get the objector's commitment of overall approval.

Experienced objection handlers bring about agreement not with pressure but with reexplanation and with persuasion that is more intellectual than emotional. They never rush the process; time is always on their side.

Managers who take the point of view that they're the boss and what they say goes risk mere surface agreement on the part of their subordinates. When this happens, it's likely that performance will be only halfhearted and the results short of objectives. It's better to spend the time in bringing about agreement than to spend it in correcting poor performance.

Employees handled in this manner will respond better to you and will be much happier and more cooperative. And so will you.

○ ○ ○ ○ ○ ○ ○ ○ ○ ○ ○ ○ ○ ○ ○ ○ ○ ○ ○ ○

105

A Shot Across the Bow

In naval parlance, a shot across the bow is a warning, not an invitation to fight. Old-time naval commanders used the warning to advise other vessels to change course or "lie to" for boarding and inspection. Until the supersonic age, this was standard operating procedure. And it was a procedure that was clearly understood by all seafarers.

You can learn something from that. When you find an employee being careless, doing poor-quality work, or behaving improperly, say something about such activity now. If employees are not warned about such irregularities, they begin to believe that what they're doing is quite acceptable. Rather than let that happen, try a shot across the bow.

Katie handles some vital sales accounts. For the most part, she writes profitable business and makes her calls on schedule. Occasionally, however, she submits an incorrect order or doesn't process it through the system as quickly as she should. Knowing that Katie is ordinarily an effective sales rep and extremely sensitive to criticism, her manager hesitates to make too many waves with her.

On previous occasions, the handling of such issues has often resulted in Katie's becoming extremely upset or threatening to quit. That's because her boss unthinkingly fires broadsides rather than mild shots across the bow. Here's how such a warning shot might be fired to bring about desired results:

You: Katie, it isn't often that I have to bring problems to your attention, because you're an outstanding rep and usually handle things well. I was surprised to get some flak from your contact at XYZ Company the other day that there was a problem on one of your deals. Can you fill me in on it?

Katie: Yes. I promised them some information on a contract matter and got tied up on some other things and didn't get back to them as promptly as I should have. It's all taken care of now. Is that what they told you?

You: That's about it. The problem was promptness—that's all. You're sure it's handled, or do you want me to get in on it?

Katie: I assure you it's handled. And I also assure you that it won't happen again.

That was a shot across the bow, intended to stop, not sink, the other ship. It began with a compliment—an acknowledgment of Katie's customarily excellent performance. It was specific in identifying a particular problem. It indicated confidence in Katie and her ability to get things back on track. It didn't belabor the issue, but it was clear in its message that management was aware and cared—cared for Katie as well as for doing business the right way.

Constructive and considerate warnings not only change an employee's behavior but also help preserve a good relationship with that employee. Equally important, early warnings prevent the need for more severe corrective action later on.

○ ○ ○ ○ ○ ○ ○ ○ ○ ○ ○ ○ ○ ○ ○ ○ ○ ○ ○ ○

106

Constructive Criticism

One of the more distasteful responsibilities of a manager is to criticize unsatisfactory behavior or performance. Make no mistake about it, it has to be done. When it isn't, the employee has every right to believe that what he or she is doing is perfectly acceptable.

Quarterly, semiannual, or annual performance reviews should be almost perfunctory, containing no dramatically new ideas or surprises for the employee. It's better to give ongoing critique or correction, as well as compliments, whenever they are indicated than to wait for review dates.

There are four cardinal rules about criticism:

1. *Attack the problem, not the person.* "You didn't do that right" attacks the person. "The better way to do that would be . . ." attacks the problem. "You should have . . ." attacks the person. "What should have been done . . ." attacks the problem. Think about the difference before you launch your next one-on-one session with an employee.

2. *Make clear what behavior or performance is acceptable and why.* "It's important that every sales report contain lost sales as well as actual orders written" is specific about desired action. Then continue, "By knowing what *didn't* sell, we can make adjustments in product or prices or terms that will result in more sales."

3. *Delineate steps to bring about the desired condition.* "Here's what should be done [note, we didn't say, "Here is what you should do . . ."] whenever a call is made that results in a no-sale. Brief explanations of why the sale didn't fly should be included." Now the rep knows the rules—where the sidelines are and the goal line is.

4. *Conclude the criticism so that it will result in the employee's commitment to change.* "Does that make sense?" "Can we count on that in the future?" When people make commitments, they tend to fulfill

them. And they do so with understanding as well as with a sense of obligation.

Constructive criticism not only stops a bad practice but initiates a good one.

○ ○

107

When Simple Correcting Fails

It happens in the best of families—the loose cannon or the impossible brat who simply can't stay in line. You'll meet one somewhere along the line—only one if you're lucky and more if you're not. Before you complain too loud, bear in mind that when an employee fails to behave, in many cases you've failed too.

I've always been such a positive thinker about motivation and leading versus driving that I've generally given very little thought to discipline. Motivation in my mind has always been a matter of finding the right reward for good performance and behavior. One day in a conference I was leading, a conferee raised this question: "When you've done all the good things you've just covered—and they don't work—what type of penalty do you apply?"

"In my mind a penalty can be defined as the absence of a reward," I replied. "Think of it this way. When you didn't do what you were supposed to do as a kid, there were a few ways of punishing you: You got a spanking, or you couldn't go out to play, or you didn't get your allowance, or when pie was served for dessert, your piece was left in the kitchen. Except for the spanking—which you can't do with adults—all the other penalties subtracted a reward."

When we looked at the things people want most as motivating factors, I mentioned tangible and intangible rewards. If your poor performer or bad actor doesn't toe the line, consider the same things—in reverse. If money is his or her motivator, hold back a raise. If recognition is the motivator, cut the offender off that list. If this is a person who revels in a promotion, postpone it a bit. In all cases, however, be sure to explain what you're doing and why you're doing it. And certainly always precede any penalty with a solid effort at counseling.

Give first-time offenders lighter penalties than repeaters, but be careful not to deal too lightly with any offense because that's an implicit invitation to repeat it. What you do to an individual will be known throughout the organization, so if Jack gets away with something, Jill might try it too.

Distinguish between actions on the part of an employee that are mistakes and those that are outright challenges to your authority. Caution mistakes and correct them with added training and coaching. Meet challenges differently: Go nose to nose with the challenger, because that's part of your job as a manager, like it or not.

There are a bunch of steps in these cases. First, keep an eye open for problems. Next, counsel and correct. When that fails, face up to discipline. If that doesn't work, ready the employee for a long walk on the outside.

If you don't like to discipline, learn to manage *very* well.

○ ○ ○ ○ ○ ○ ○ ○ ○ ○ ○ ○ ○ ○ ○ ○ ○ ○ ○ ○

108

The Day I Turned the Boss Around

"I turned the boss around today," said Chuck. "He wanted me to drop everything and get onto one of his pet projects, and I simply said *no*." "And what did *he* say?" asked Mrs. Chuck. "He told me clean out my desk," said Chuck as he handed his wife a box of pencils, pens, paper clips, and a potted fern.

Make no mistake about it—the quickest way to find yourself up-dating résumés is to tell the boss to go bag it. Yet there are times when bosses are wrong. What they want done can't be done when and how they want it, or doing it at all would be a business error. Employees have not only the right but the responsibility to change a manager's mind if that manager is heading in a wrong direction. But, please, don't just say *no*!

Here are a few alternatives if you want to maintain a healthy and continuing relationship with your boss:

> "I understand the assignment, and I'll handle it. I do, however, have minor problems with some details. Can we talk about a few of them?"
>
> "I'm a little surprised to hear you want to launch that program so early. I'll have to rearrange some other assignments in favor of an early launch. Is the date you just mentioned firm, or is it adjustable?"
>
> "Is that the same project we postponed last year for lack of budget? Do we have the money to go ahead with it now?"
>
> "You know, since we talked about this the last time, some new technology has become available. Can we talk about that?"

In all of the responses is tacit acceptance of an order to do something. Then, without actually saying that the assignment is wrong, the job can't be done, there isn't enough time or money, or the old plan is passé, there are hints in that direction. The opening statement sets aside or mutes negative tone; the follow-up comment initiates discussion of the pros and cons of the assignment.

Many managers fall into a habit of issuing orders without prior discussion. This is what participative management tries to avoid, but even in that environment there are surprises. Another habit of managers is to express an interest or desire that sounds like, "Drop everything and get on this *right now*." *Right now* may really mean *next month*. Wisdom dictates that you had better know which is which.

Arguing with your boss is only a touch better than saying *no* and being tossed out on your ear. Better still is accepting the assignment and refining it to your liking. What can happen as the discussion goes on is a broad change in the original concept or even dropping it in favor of the alternative you put forth—with the boss's help, of course.

○ ○ ○ ○ ○ ○ ○ ○ ○ ○ ○ ○ ○ ○ ○ ○ ○ ○ ○ ○

109

Time Out

The Bible narrative of the Creation tells us that God rested when it was accomplished. Whatever your theological point of view, the point is clear: There's a time for work and a time when both body and mind need a change of pace. Blow a whistle, ring a bell, lock the place up. It's time-out.

Some managers, dedicated to their jobs, carry home a briefcase full of material each evening and spend weekends bent over work-related tasks. There may be many reasons for this: The job is too big, the manager isn't well organized, work that should have been delegated hasn't been, emergencies occur that require special attention, and so on. I've known managers who wend their way to the office on Saturdays and Sundays, and their only departure from the weekly routine is to get there an hour late, and minus a tie.

Working hard is laudable. Taking work home some evenings may not be all bad. Spending an off-day at the office doesn't necessarily stamp one as a workaholic. But when this becomes a way of life, it raises some serious questions. Why is it necessary? What's wrong with the job? What's wrong with the manager? And what is this extra pressure doing to the individual? Equally important, what does this sort of nonsense mean to others in the organization?

Herb was an admitted workaholic. His family knew him primarily as the guy who brought them a paycheck once a month. If he didn't take off for the office on Saturday morning, he spent a good part of the day in his study, writing and making telephone calls. When he took a vacation, he did so only to minimize family arguments and even then he called his office two or three times a day.

You might say that what Herb did was his business and nobody else's. But what Herb did was call his subordinates in the evening and on weekends. "I was looking over the ABC contract, and I need some information from you." For Herb, waiting until the next day was a waste of time, and didn't everyone share his zeal for work? The answer was *no*, and while a few individuals catered to his whims, others hid on weekends or quit.

Time off is important—if not for yourself, then for others. Demand a full day's work for a full day's pay, but respect employees' private lives and personal time. There's a difference in working things out and wearing things out.

○ ○ ○ ○ ○ ○ ○ ○ ○ ○ ○ ○ ○ ○ ○ ○ ○ ○ ○ ○

110

Are You Well Represented?

Managers are identified with the people they employ and to whom they delegate responsibilities. Anyone in your department who has any interface with other organizations, in or out of the company, is you in the eyes of those they meet. Have someone handle your correspondence or send an employee to a meeting you're unable to attend, and that person represents not only your department but you.

As is true in so many things, we don't think of this as a serious matter until something goes wrong. Then we either have to defend the subordinate or apologize for him or her. How much better it is to cultivate employees to function in a manner that represents you and your department properly. Interpersonal and interdepartmental relationships are vital to you; make them work at all times and in all situations.

Field sales managers know this. When they try to salvage an account one of their reps has lost, they find buyers as hostile to them as they were to the rep. Or take it inside the company. Marcia has a paycheck problem and calls payroll. A clerk there treats her shabbily. Marcia has nothing good to say about the payroll department, even though she has had a bad experience with only one person there. If you're the manager of that department, you inherit Marcia's wrath despite the fact that, had she talked to you, you would have treated her with courtesy and concern.

The most annoying of these relationship breakdowns are often the simple, everyday behaviors of employees. Take telephone answering, for example. Curt, unresponsive telephone manners are seen as *your* manners because *you* approve of them. You don't approve? That's funny; we think you do, because you allow them to persist.

I recall occasionally calling a manager in another department in the company. His secretary would answer, "X Department" in an unfriendly voice. "May I speak to Mr. Thompson?" I'd ask. "Who's calling?" was the crisp reply. After hearing this a few times, I spoke to Thompson about it. He said, "Well, that's Patty for you."

The next time I called, I got the same reception. In answer to "Who's calling?" I lowered my voice and said, "This is the White House—Washington. Urgent." A long pause. Thompson came on the line with, "Yes, *sir*." When I told him why I did what I did, he laughed and said, "I get the point." After that, reception was more polite. "Mr. Thompson's office . . . Yes he's in, may I tell him who's calling?" That was true not only with his secretary but throughout the department.

Sell the idea of representation by making it clear to every employee that he or she represents every other person in the department—not just you. You, of course, will get most of the credit; it's your department that will earn the label as a sharp operation.

○ ○

111

Give Some Credit Away

In your role as manager, there are people who help you and make you look good. You, in turn, often make your boss look good. Never hesitate to acknowledge contributions by slipping in a compliment here and there to settle the debt. Even the most meager of acknowledgments may pave the way for improved performances by yourself as well as by others.

Let's say you submit a proposal to management that meets with considerable acceptance. *Never* neglect to credit those people who dug up the data and nursed it through a half-dozen revisions to produce that proposal. My local newspaper now gives bylines not only to writers but to reporters who fed information to the article. It's an easy thing you can do to generate effective relationships.

Giving credit up and across is equally important. Suppose you're trying to sell an idea to your boss and remember that it was her suggestion that got you going in the first place. "Remember our conversation regarding . . .? You got me thinking about possible solutions to that problem, and I'd like to play off a few ideas with you." She'd be an interpersonal relations zero if she wouldn't take time to listen to ideas she helped trigger in the first place.

Suppose that you manage advertising, and another person runs the sales organization. This is a synergism of sorts; it takes ads to promote sales, and salespeople have ideas about advertising. You go to your sales counterpart and suggest that the two of you plan a new-product introduction effort. The invitation is accepted. Your sales associate offers some ideas, and you work up ads, brochures, mailers, catalogs, and point-of-sale devices.

If you two managers are smart, you'll be generous with credit to one another. When told that your ad campaign is a winner, say, "I got terrific input from . . ." And when the sales manager hits record sales, he or she should say, "We benefited from a good ad campaign."

You don't rob from your own success by crediting an employee, a superior, or a peer. In fact, what you may find is greater cooperation from others that ensures even greater success for yourself.

○ ○ ○ ○ ○ ○ ○ ○ ○ ○ ○ ○ ○ ○ ○ ○ ○ ○ ○

112

The Secret Is in How You Say It

You can create good relationships with employees by learning to say things correctly. It isn't so much the words you say but the way you put those words together. The content of a message may be important, but how you say it is the secret to smooth relationships and, equally important, desired responses.

A simple example is in saying *yes* or *no*. There are cases in which a question or a request can be answered with a single word: *yes* or *no*. "Would you like these files left out?" "Yes." "Would you like more coffee?" "No." Add *please* and *thank you*, of course. You seldom need clarifying statements to answer questions like these. The simple and brief will do.

Not all questions are so simple. Try this one: "I have two errands to run that can't be handled evenings or weekends. May I take this afternoon off to handle them?" If you would reply *yes* to this request, your answer should include some explanation. Why are you willing to approve a half-day's absence? Don't you care? Is the employee's presence unimportant? Or do you feel the employee has earned special favors of this sort? Unless you add explanation, you aren't culturing the relationship. This might work: "Yes, Bill, go ahead and handle your business; there are times when such things can't be avoided. And I appreciate your asking in advance so that we can cover for you if any calls come in. We'll see you in the morning." Bill can now leave without feeling he has incurred your disapproval. And treatment of this sort minimizes game playing and using sick days as absence excuses.

Now suppose you can't let Bill off this afternoon, and your answer must be *no*. The way you say it will make a big difference in how Bill reacts to the refusal: "This is a particularly bad afternoon, Bill. I'm going to be attending a planning meeting downtown, and we have three client proposals to get out first thing in the morning. We really need everyone on hand to handle the load. I'm afraid I'll have to say no. Can you plan your calls for tomorrow or later in the week?" Bill may not like what you have said to him, but he knows why, and he can't complain about how you said it.

Notice the difference in the two answers. When saying *yes*, you give approval first and then explain. When saying *no*, you give the explanation prior to refusing. Good news first . . . bad news last. This is equally true in written messages. If you have to deal with customers or other departments within your company, get into this habit of saying it right.

Everyone around you will appreciate it!

○ ○ ○ ○ ○ ○ ○ ○ ○ ○ ○ ○ ○ ○ ○ ○ ○ ○ ○ ○

113

Finish Line or Firing Line?

Many years ago, I was teaching a management course in public speaking and assigned as a speech topic, "A Work Relationship Problem I Faced—and Solved." The managers not only had some interesting situations, but their handling of them showed considerable insight. The last speaker of the afternoon stole the show.

The allotted time was four minutes. He went on for three and one-half minutes describing a boss he once had who broke every rule in the human relations book. I was about to signal the speaker to watch his time when he said, "And so you wonder how I solved this problem. [*Dramatic pause.*] I quit!" *Thunderous laugh.* Class dismissed!

That was one way to solve the problem. Another way relationship problems are solved is to fire employees. The first may be called the finish line, and the last can be called the firing line. While you may not think you have much control over quits, you do. And while you may believe you're in the driver's seat with fires, you may be surprised at the difficulties you face there.

People quit for a variety of reasons, but one thing is sure: They'd rather work someplace else than for you—better job, more pay, better hours, job closer to home. You may not be in a position to counteract these elements, but there's one more you should be concerned about: How did you get along?

When employees quit over poor relationships with managers, the word gets around, inside and outside the company. Your turnover rate may have a lot to do with your rating upstairs. Leaving for a better job is explainable; leaving for a better manager isn't. Conduct exit interviews with employees who leave, and learn what you might have done to cause the leaving or to have prevented it.

Firing is different. It's one of the more distasteful things a manager must do from time to time. Frequently an employee's failure is a manager's failure—but not always. The mistake you might have made with the person you're saying goodbye to may have been back in the hiring process. Be careful with firing because there are backlashes that can cause you real trouble.

Watch out for age and sex discrimination. Some such problems are real, but some get invented as the fired hand goes out the door. Take time in firing anyone; collect evidence of poor performance, spotty attendance, destructive behavior, and other work-related problems. Note times, dates, and types of discussions you've had with the employee. Be sure you have done a pile of constructive acts before resorting to firing.

One thing we know: Managers who coach employees to good performance and counsel them to good behavior are managers who see little of either the finish line or the firing line. Maintaining effective worker relationships is more fun than conducting exit interviews anyhow.

○ ○

114

Are You Listening?

Unless curricula have changed drastically in the last few years, it's likely that you've never really had any serious instruction in the art of listening. The assumption is that listening is a natural and simple act and that courses on it in schools and colleges aren't needed. But listening is important—not only in grasping what others say but in relationships between co-workers and managers.

There aren't very many good listeners. The gut issues are not in hearing but in the attention given, the ability to sift relevant from irrelevant, and controlling emotions during the process.

Let's suppose you're sitting in a meeting and your boss is outlining a policy change. Do your level best to block out your other concerns—the report that's due first thing in the morning and the problem at home with the water heater. Important as these are, they aren't the issues at the moment. Paying attention is the first rule of listening.

Listen for key points, not nuts and bolts. You'll get the details later when the policy is issued. And don't begin to make up questions and comments until you've heard the whole story. Apply these rules when listening to your boss in a meeting and also to listening to an employee in your office.

The challenge to listeners is to listen carefully, listen for key ideas and fill in the details as needed, and do their best to put emotions in neutral while in the process. And *don't* interrupt either. Use this sequence:

- Receive first. Take it all in, period.
- Understand second. Tie ideas and facts together.
- Make judgments third. Reflect and consider.
- Respond last. What you say will make sense.

Be a good listener. You'll learn a lot, you'll make better decisions, and you'll make more friends, too.

○ ○ ○ ○ ○ ○ ○ ○ ○ ○ ○ ○ ○ ○ ○ ○ ○ ○ ○ ○

115

Maintenance vs. Repair

Automobile owners know that spending money on maintenance often obviates the need for costly repairs. Car companies know that, too, and many warranty clauses hinge on evidence of maintenance done during the coverage period. The same idea applies to the care and keeping of business organizations. Don't let once-established effective relationships deteriorate; they're harder to repair than to maintain.

People in plant management know that and walk the shop often to make their presence known, as well as to observe what's going on. They stop and talk to people. They listen to them. They make sure of safety and health factors beyond federal demands. They attend to people in the same way they attend to production. Maintenance.

Sales managers go into the field and work with reps. They bring reps in from time to time for training and for personal contact. They interface with customers just to keep abreast of the marketplace and its problems. Maintenance.

The same holds true for purchasing, finance, engineering, personnel, advertising—or whatever else your organization does: The people involved deserve attention as much as the tools they work with. If you schedule maintenance for computers, forklifts, trucks, conveyor lines, or just pencil sharpeners, schedule checkups and adjustments for folks who run them. Maintenance.

Scheduling doesn't mean haphazard or chance meetings with people in the corridors or in the parking lot. Arrange to sit down individually or in group meetings with everyone in your organization from time to time. Before you say that can't be done, let's look at the real facts of management life:

• Few of us manage directly more than ten or twenty people. Often it's only five or six. In a one-hundred-person department, the top gun may have a staff of six, and they in turn supervise ten, fifteen, or twenty. The arithmetic may vary, but the concept remains similar.

• If you're at the top, you meet with key people on routine business frequently but also schedule time with them on a regular basis, and singly.

• With the example you set with your own group, encourage members to do the same with their subordinates. If that isn't possible, have them hold short meetings, on the line or in the field. Maybe these are for giving out instructions or news, but they should also solicit ideas and questions from participants.

We examine machine parts and lubricate them regularly. Why not apply the same reasoning to the people who run them? We set aside time for annual reviews for performance and compensation purposes. Why not a few interim meetings to prevent surprises later on? This is neither pampering nor tampering—just plain good sense and good management. It makes good people better—a neat swap for a few minutes of your time.

○ ○

A Postscript

Postscripts serve one of two useful functions: They add things not covered earlier or point up thoughts requiring particular emphasis. Since I have no intention of adding anything, only "particular emphasis" remains on the agenda.

Every industry, every company, every job is different. You may manage in a climate and in circumstances different from those I've described here. One thing remains constant, however, and that's your mandate to bring about the best performance you know how from the people you manage. Your job is to lead and to help. That's right, to *help*. Just as this book has emphasized little things, so you'll find that little helps result in big accomplishments.

Managing is more than a job; it's an adventure. Go to your place of work each day with an eye to discovering new ways in which to affect the lives and achievements of others. To be sure, you'll meet up with problems and disappointments, but you'll also meet up with successes: the project you finish that others said couldn't be done or the worker you turn from uninspired to enthusiastic. Little things.

What you know is important. What you do with what you know is even more important! Get going . . . and a happy adventure!

Index